How to speak Japanese

Editors Hiroshi Takahashi
Kyoko Takahashi
the chief editor Tomoko Honjo

TAISEIDO

Title: How to speak Japanese © *1995*
Taiseido Shobo Co.
Tokyo & Kobe, Japan

Preface

This book is for Japanese learners. In Part 1 emphasis is placed on conjugation on main verbs and auxiliaries with illustration and explanation; Part 2 consists of daily conversations; and in Part 3, the way of counting objects is shown. At the end, words concerning the human body and medical care are given.

It is our hope that though this is a small book, it will help beginners of the Japanese language to learn and master Japanese. We will be very happy if you readers use this book repeatedly as a reference when the need arises.

Editors Hiroshi Takahashi
Kyoko Takahashi

the chief editor Tomoko Honjô

GUIDES

The following points should be noted as to guides to Romanized Japanese.

(1) The Romanized Letters are used according to the system of the attached table.

(2) ^ on the vowel marks "long vowel."

ex. make up	keshô-o-suru

(3) A geminated consonant is represented by the double consonant letters. However,「っち」is represented by *tchi*, not *cchi*.

ex. went	itta
accord	itchi-suru

(4) The syllabic nasal is represented by **m**, which is placed before *b, m. p.*

ex. A-bomb	ge**m***b*aku
advisable	ke**m***m*ei-na
advanced	shi**m***p*o-shita

(5) When a vowel or a sound in the '*y*' or '*a*' series of the Kana syllabary follows a syllabic nasal, ' is placed to make the syllabic boundary clear.

ex. credit shin'yô
dear shin'ai-na
cause gen'in
dark in'utsu-na
prosperity han'ei
disgust ken'o

References to the Romanized Letters

the	a	series	a	i	u	e	o
〃	k	〃	k·a	k·i	k·u	k·e	k·o
〃	g	〃	g·a	g·i	g·u	g·e	g·o
〃	s	〃	s·a	sh·i	s·u	s·e	s·o
〃	z	〃	z·a	j·i	z·u	z·e	z·o
〃	t	〃	t·a	ch·i	ts·u	t·e	t·o
〃	d	〃	d·a			d·e	d·o
〃	n	〃	n·a	n·i	n·u	n·e	n·o
〃	h	〃	h·a	h·i	f·u	h·e	h·o
〃	b	〃	b·a	b·i	b·u	b·e	b·o
〃	p	〃	p·a	p·i	p·u	p·e	p·o
〃	m	〃	m·a	m·i	m·u	m·e	m·o
〃	y	〃	y·a	(i)	y·u	(e)	y·o
〃	r	〃	r·a	r·i	r·u	r·e	r·o

〃	w	〃	w·a	(i)	(u)	(e)	(o)
〃	n	〃					
			kya		kyu		kyo
			gya		gyu		gyo
			sha		shu	she	sho
			ja		ju	je	jo
			cha		chu	che	cho
			nya		nyu		nyo
			hya		hyu		hyo
			bya		byu		byo
			pya		pyu		pyo
			mya		myu		myo
			rya		ryu		ryo
				di			
			fa	fi		fe	fo
				ti			
				wi		we	wo

A table of contents

PART 1. The conjugation on main verbs and auxiliaries 1

The table of conjugation of verbs 30

The table of conjugation of auxiliaries 54

PART 2. Daily conversation 62

1) Time (jikan) 63
2) Climate (Tenkô) 65
3) A weather forecast (Tenki-yohô) 66
4) At the immigration office (Shutsu-nyûgoku-kanri-jimu-sho-de) 68
5) At the customs (Zeikan-de) 68
6) Being greeted (Demukae) 69
7) Self-introduction (Jiko-shôkai) 70
8) Introduction (Shôkai) 71
9) Visiting someone (Hômon) 72
10) Visiting someone at an office (Kaisha-ni hito-o tazuneru) 75
11) Leaving one's home (O-itoma) 76
12) Hotel reservation (Hoteru-no yoyaku) 77
13) At the hotel (Hoteru-de) 79
14) Asking the way (Michi-o tazuneru) 80
15) At a station (Eki-de) 84

16) In a train (Shanai-de) 86
17) Tickets (Kippu) 87
18) Doing the sights (Kankô) 89
19) Cars (Kuruma) 93
20) A photograph (Shashin) 94
21) Meals (Shokuji) 97
22) Shopping (Kai-mono) 99
23) Complaints (Kujô) 107
24) A phone (Denwa) 108
25) Making an arrangement (Yakusoku) 113
26) At the office (Jimu-sho-de) 114
27) After work (Shigoto-no-ato-de) 115
28) At a hospital (Byôin-de) 116
29) At the post office (Yûbin-kyoku-de) 121

PART 3. The way of counting the objects 123

PART 4. The human body and medical care ... 151

The conjugation on main verbs and auxiliaries

All the verbs and two auxiliaries are indicated in boldface and some of them are underlined. In these cases, only underlined parts conjugate.

Clean (sôji-suru) is a compound verb which is formed with a noun of Chinese origin(sôji) and the verb suru. Another examples are 'make sure' (kakunin-suru) and 'chat' (zatsudan-suru) etc. A loan word may be used in the same manner (e.g. 'set' setto-suru). See suru in the table in such cases.

Tables of conjugation are given at the end of this Part. (Please) Refer to them.

1) I **get up** early in the morning.

   Watashi-wa asa haya-ku **o-k·iru**. [Refer to 9)]

2) I **open** the windows.

   Watashi-wa mado-o **a-k·eru**. [Refer to 10).]

3) I **go** to the bathroom.

   Watashi-wa toire-ni **i-k·u**. [Refer to 1).]

4) I **brush** my teeth.

   Watashi-wa ha-o **miga-k·u**. [Refer to 1).]

5) I **wash** my face.

   Watashi-wa kao-o **ara-u**. [Refer to 8).]

6) I **brush** my teeth **and wash** my face.

Watashi-wa ha-o **miga-k·i** or **miga-i-te** kao-o **ara-u**. [Refer to 1) & 8).]

7) I **rinse out** my mouth.

Watashi-wa kuchi-o **susu-g·u**. [Refer to 2).]

8) I **gargle**.

Watashi-wa **ugai-o-suru**. [Refer to 11).]

9) I **shave**.

Watashi-wa **hige-o-so-r·u**. [Refer to 7).]

10) I **don't shave**.

Watashi-wa **hige-o-so-r·a-na-i**. [Refer to 7).]

11) I **put on** my shirt.

Watashi-wa shatsu-o **k·iru**. [Refer to 9).]

12) I **put on** my pants.

Watashi-wa zubon-o **ha-k·u**. [Refer to 1).]

13) She **puts on** her skirt.

Kano-jo-wa sukâto-o **ha-k·u**. [Refer to 1).]

14) I **comb** my hair.

Watashi-wa kami-o **kushi-de-to-k·u**. [Refer to 1).]

15) She **makes up**.

Kano-jo-wa **keshô-o-suru**. [Refer to 11).]

16) I **put** some water in a kettle.

Watashi-wa yakan-ni mizu-o **i-r·eru**. [Refer to 10).]

17) I **put** the kettle on the gas range.

Watashi-wa yakan-o gasu-renji-ni **ka-k·eru**. [Refer to 10).]

18) I **boil** some water.

Watashi-wa yu-o **waka-s·u**. [Refer to 3).]

19) She **chops** cabbage.

Kano-jo-wa kyabetsu-o **kiza-m·u**. [Refer to 6).]

20) She **wants** to make salad.

Kano-jo-wa sarada-o tsuku-ri-**tai**. [Refer to aux. 4).]

21) I **make** fried eggs.

Watashi-wa medama-yaki-o **tsuku-r·u**. [Refer to 6).]

22) I **toast** bread.

Watashi-wa pan-o **ya-k·u**. [Refer to 1).]

23) I **make** coffee.

Watashi-wa kôhî-o **waka-s·u**. [Refer to 3).]

24) I **spread** butter on toast.

Watashi-wa tôsuto-ni batâ-o **nu-r·u**. [Refer to 7).]

25) She **puts** dressing on a green salad.

Kano-jo-wa gurîn-sarada-ni doresshingu-o **ka-k·eru**. [Refer to 10).]

26) I **put** sugar and milk in my coffee.

Watashi-wa kôhî-ni satô to miruku-o **i-r·eru**. [Refer to 10).]

27) I **stir** milk in my coffee.

Watashi-wa kôhî-ni miruku-o-ire-te (supun-de) **ma-z·eru**. [Refer to 10).]

28) I **read** the newspaper.

Watashi-wa shimbun-o **yo-m·u**. [Refer to 6).]

29) I **polish** my shoes.

Watashi-wa kutsu-o **miga-k·u**. [Refer to 1).]

30) I **put on** a tie.

Watashi-wa nekutai-o **shi-m·eru**. [Refer to 10).]

31) I **put on** my jacket.

Watashi-wa uwagi-o **k·iru**. [Refer to 9).]

32) I **put on** my shoes.

Watashi-wa kutsu-o **ha-k·u**. [Refer to 1).]

33) She **sends** two children to the kindergarten.

Kano-jo-wa futari-no kodomo(-tachi)-o yôchi-en-ni **oku-r·u**. [Refer to 7).]

34) She **runs** the washing machine.

Kano-jo-wa sentakki-o **mawa-s·u**. [Refer to 3).]

35) She **takes** the laundry *out of* the washing machine.

Kano-jo-wa sentakki-kara sentaku-mono-o **tori-da-s·u**. [Refer to 3).]

36) She **hangs out** the laundry on a clothesline.

Kano-jo-wa sentaku-mono-o mono-hoshi-zuna-ni **ho-s·u**. [Refer to 3).]

37) She **airs** the bedding(=futon) in the sun.

Kano-jo-wa futon-o **ho-s·u**. [Refer to 3).]

38) She **tidies up** the room.

Kano-jo-wa heya-o **katazu-k·eru**. [Refer to 10).]

39) She **vacuums** the floor.

Kano-jo-wa yuka-ni **sôji-ki-o-ka-k·eru**. [Refer to 10).]

40) She **wipes** the floor.

Kano-jo-wa yuka-o **fu-k·u**. [Refer to 1).]

41) She **clears** the table.

Kano-jo-wa têburu-o **katazu-k·eru**. [Refer to 10).]

42) She **washes** the dishes.

Kano-jo-wa sara-o **ara-u**. [Refer to 8).]

43) She **stands** the dishes *against* a rack.

Kano-jo-wa sara-o rakku-ni **tate-ka-k·eru**. [Refer to 10).]

44) She **gathers up** garbage (from the kitchen).

Kano-jo-wa (daidokoro-kara) gomi-o **atsu-m·eru**. [Refer to 10).]

45) She **cleans** the bathtub.

Kano-jo-wa yokusô-o **sôji-suru**. [Refer to 11).]

46) She **turns off** the gas.

Kano-jo-wa gasu(-no-motosen)-o **shi-m·eru**. [Refer to 10).]

47) She **switches off** the light.

Kano-jo-wa denki-o **ke-s·u**. [Refer to 3).]

48) She **locks** the front door.

Kano-jo-wa genkan-no **kagi-o-ka-k·eru**. [Refer to 10).]

49) She **goes** shopping to a supermarket.

Kano-jo-wa sûpâ-e kaimono-ni-**i-k·u**. [Refer to 1).]

50) She **rides** a bicycle.

Kano-jo-wa jitensha-ni **no-r·u**. [Refer to 7).]

51) She **puts** a shopping basket on a cart.

Kano-jo-wa kâto-ni kaimono-kago-o **no-s·eru**. [Refer to 10).]

52) She **chooses** fresh fish.

Kano-jo-wa shinsen-na sakana-o **era-b·u**. [Refer to 5).]

53) She **checks** her shopping list.

Kano-jo-wa kaimono-memo-o **m·i-ru**. [Refer to 9).]

54) She **waits** in the check-out line.

Kano-jo-wa reji-de **ma-ts·u**. [Refer to 4).]

55) She **pays** at the check-out counter.

Kano-jo-wa reji-de **seisan-suru**. [Refer to 11).]

56) She **receives** change and a receipt.

Kano-jo-wa o-tsuri to reshîto-o **uke-to-r·u**. [Refer to 7).]

57) She **makes sure** if she got the right change.

Kano-jo-wa tsuri-sen-o **kakunin-suru**. [Refer to 11).]

58) She **puts** her purchases in a plastic bag.

Kano-jo-wa katta-mono-o binîru-bukuro-ni **i-r·eru**. [Refer to 10).]

59) She **chats** with her neighbor.

Kano-jo-wa kinjo-no-hito-to **zatsudan-suru**. [Refer to 11).]

60) She **uses** a telephone card for a public phone.

Kano-jo-wa kôshû-denwa-o-kakeru-tame-ni terehon-kâdo-o **tsuka-u**. [Refer to 8).]

61) She **puts** a 100 yen coin in the vending machine.

Kano-jo-wa jidô-hambai-ki-ni hyaku-en-dama-o **i-r·eru**. [Refer to 10).]

62) She **pushes** a button of the vending machine.

Kano-jo-wa jidô-hambai-ki no botan-o **o-s·u**. [Refer to 3).]

63) She **takes** the can of juice *out of* the vending machine.

Kano-jo-wa jidô-hambai-ki-kara jûsu no kan-o **tori-da-s·u**. [Refer to 3).]

64) She **puts** her package in a bicycle-basket.

Kano-jo-wa jitensha-no-kago-ni nimotsu-o **i-r·eru**. [Refer to 10).]

65) She **unlocks** the front door.

Kano-jo-wa genkan-no to-no **kagi-o-a-k·eru**. [Refer to 10).]

66) She **unloads** purchases at the entrance hall.

Kano-jo-wa genkan-ni katta-mono-o **oro-s·u**. [Refer to 3).]

67) She **takes off** her shoes.

Kano-jo-wa kutsu-o **nu-g·u**. [Refer to 2).]

68) She **puts** frozen food in the freezer part of the refrigerator.

Kano-jo-wa reizô-ko no reitô-shitsu-ni reitô-hin-o **i-r·eru**. [Refer to 10).]

69) She **takes** the laundry *from* the line.

Kano-jo-wa mono-hoshi-zuna-kara sentaku-mono-o **tori-ko-m·u**. [Refer to 6).]

70) She **irons** the clothes.

Kano-jo-wa irui-ni **airon-o-ka-k·eru**. [Refer to 10).]

71) She **takes** a nap.

Kano-jo-wa utatane-o **suru**. [Refer to 11).]

72) She **goes and picks** the kids from the kindergarten.
Kano-jo-wa yôchi-en-ni kodomo-o **mukae-ni-i-k·u**. [Refer to 1).]

73) She **gives** them a snack.
Kano-jo-wa kare-ra-ni oyatsu-o **ata-eru**. [Refer to 10).]

74) She **takes care** of her child's friend(s).
Kano-jo-wa kodomo-no tomodachi-o **azuka-r·u**. [Refer to 7).]

75) A phone **is ringing**.
Denwa-ga **natte-iru**. [Refer to 9).]

76) He **picks up** the receiver.
Kare-wa juwa-ki-o **to-r·u**. [Refer to 7).]

77) He **makes** a long phone call.
Kare-wa naga-denwa-o **suru**. [Refer to 11).]

78) He **talks** this and that.
Kare-wa are-kore **hanashi-o-suru**. [Refer to 11).]

79) She **answers** the interphone.
Kano-jo-wa intâhon-ni **d·eru**. [Refer to 10).]

80) A friend **came** to see me.
Tomodachi-ga asobi-ni **ki-ta**. [Refer to 12).]

81) I **serve** a guest tea.

Watashi-wa o-kyaku-ni o-cha-o **da-s·u**. [Refer to 3).]

82) I **cut** a cake.

Watashi-wa kêki-o **ki-r·u**. [Refer to 7).]

83) I **went** to see a friend.

Watashi-wa tomodachi-ni ai-ni **itta**. [Refer to 1).]

84) I **bought** a small present.

Watashi-wa te-miyage-o **katta**. [Refer to 8).]

85) I **prepared** supper.

Watashi-wa yûshoku-no **yôi-o-shi-ta**. [Refer to 11).]

86) I **fried** meat in a frying pan.

Watashi-wa furai-pan-de niku-o **ita-m·e-ta**. [Refer to 10).]

87) I **cooked** some curry.

Watashi-wa karê-o **ni-ko-n-da**. [Refer to 6).]

88) I **cooked** rice.

Watashi-wa gohan-o **ta-i-ta**. [Refer to 1).]

89) I **grilled** fish.

Watashi-wa (ami-de) sakana-o **ya-i-ta**. [Refer to

1).]

90) I **deep-fried** fish and vegetables.

Watashi-wa sakana ya yasai-o **a-g·e-ta**. [Refer to 10).]

91) My stomach **is growling**.

(Watashi-no) Onaka-ga **natte-iru**. [Refer to 9).]

92) She **turns on** a ventilation fan.

Kano-jo-wa kanki-sen-o **mawa-s·u**. [Refer to 3).]

93) She **defrosts** ... with a microwave.

Kano-jo-wa denshi-renji-de ... -o **kaitô-suru**. [Refer to 11).]

94) She **heats** ... with a microwave.

Kano-jo-wa denshi-renji-de ... -o **kanetsu-suru**. [Refer to 11).]

95) She **tastes** the seasoning of ... .

Kano-jo-wa ... no aji-**mi-o-suru**. [Refer to 11).]

96) She **seasons** ... with salty-sweet.

Kano-jo-wa ... -o ama-kara-ku **aji-tsuke-suru**. [Refer to 11).]

97) She **dishes up**.

Kano-jo-wa **ryôri-o-mori-tsu-k·eru**. [Refer to

10).]

98) She **pours** tea in a cup.

Kano-jo-wa koppu-ni o-cha-o **i-r·eru**. [Refer to 10).]

99) **Let's have** supper.

Yûshoku-o **ta-b·eyô**. [Refer to 10).]

100) We **pour** Worcester sauce (or soy sauce).

Watashi-tachi-wa sôsu-o(shôyu-o) **ka-k·eru**. [Refer to 10).]

101) I **took off** my tie.

Watashi-wa nekutai-o **hazu-sh·i-ta**. [Refer to 3).]

102) I **hung up** my suit of clothes.

Watashi-wa sûtsu-o **hangâ-ni-ka-k·e-ta**. [Refer to 10).]

103) I **turned on** a TV.

Watashi-wa terebi-o **ka-k·e-ta**. [Refer to 10).]

104) I **opened** a can beer.

Watashi-wa kan-bîru-o **a-k·e-ta**. [Refer to 10).]

105) I **changed** the channel.

Watashi-wa channeru-o **mawa-sh·i-ta**. [Refer to 3).]

106) I **turned off** the TV.

Watashi-wa terebi-o **ke-sh·i-ta**. [Refer to 3).]

107) I **listened** to the CD.

Watashi-wa shî-dî-o **ki-i-ta**. [Refer to 1).]

108) She **checked** the children's homework.

Kano-jo-wa kodomo-tachi-no shukudai-o **m·i-ta**. [Refer to 9).]

109) I **heated** the bath water.

Watashi-wa furo-o **waka-sh·i-ta**. [Refer to 3).]

110) I **took** a long slow bath.

Watashi-wa yukkuri-to furo-ni **haitta**. [Refer to 7).]

111) I **didn't take** a shower.

Watashi-wa shawâ-o **ab·i-na-katta**. [Refer to 9).]

112) I **washed myself** with a soap.

Watashi-wa sekken-de **karada-o arratta**. [Refer to 8).]

113) I **shampooed** my hair.

Watashi-wa atama-no-kami-no-ke-o **shampû-shi-ta**. [Refer to 11).]

114) I **dried** my body with a towel.

Watashi-wa taoru-de karada-o **fu-i-ta**. [Refer to 1).]

115) I **weighed myself.**

Watashi-wa **taijû-o-hakatta**. [Refer to 7).]

116) I **dried** my hair with a hair-drier.

Watashi-wa hea-doraiyâ-de atama-no-kami-no-ke-o **kawaka-sh·i-ta**. [Refer to 3).]

117) I **got ready** for the meeting tomorrow.

Watashi-wa asu-no kaigi-no **jumbi-o-shi-ta**. [Refer to 11).]

118) I **set** the alarm for 6 o'clock.

Watashi-wa mezamashi-o roku-ji-ni **setto-shi-ta**. [Refer to 11).]

119) I **take** a bus.

Watashi-wa basu-ni **no-r·u**. [Refer to 7).]

120) I **climb up** the stairs in the station.

Watashi-wa eki-de kaidan-o **nobo-r·u**. [Refer to 7).]

121) I **insert** a pass to the automatic ticket checker.

Watashi-wa kaisatsu-ki-ni teiki-o **i-r·eru**. [Refer to 10).]

122) I **stand** inside the white line at the platform.

Watashi-wa hômu-de hakusen-no-uchigawa-ni **ta-ts·u**. [Refer to 4).]

123) I **buy** a newspaper at the newsstand.

Watashi-wa baiten-de shimbun-o **ka-u**. [Refer to 8).]

124) I **get on** the train.

Watashi-wa densha-ni **no-r·u**. [Refer to 7).]

125) **If** I **get on** this train, I'**ll not be late** to the office.

(Watashi-wa) Kono densha-ni **no-r·e-ba**, kaisha-ni **chikoku-shi-na-i-da-rô**. [Refer to 7) & 11).]

126) I **run into** the train.

Watashi-wa densha-ni **tobi-no-r·u**. [Refer to 7).]

127) **If** I **miss** that train, I'**ll be late** to the office.

(Watashi-wa) Ano densha-ni **nori-oku-r·ere-ba**, kaisha-ni-**chikoku-suru-da-rô**. [Refer to 10) & 11).]

128) I **don't change** trains.

Watashi-wa densha-o **nori-ka-e-na-i**. [Refer to 10).]

129) I **hit** the rush hour.

Watashi-wa tsûkin-rasshu-ni **a-u**. [Refer to 8).]

130) **Hang on** to the strap.

Tsuri-kawa-ni **tsukama-r·e**. [Refer to 7).]

131) A young man **gave** his seat to the elderly.

Seinen-ga o-toshiyori-ni zaseki-o **yuzutta**. [Refer to 7).]

132) Automatic doors **open**.

Jidô-tobira-ga **a-k·u**. [Refer to 1).]

133) I **get off** the train.

Watashi-wa densha-o **o-r·iru**. [Refer to 9).]

134) I **go out** the ticket gate.

Watashi-wa kaisatsu-guchi-o **d·eru**. [Refer to 10).]

135) I **cross** at the cross walk.

Watashi-wa ôdan-hodô-o **wata-r·u**. [Refer to 7).]

136) I **wait** for the light to change.

Watashi-wa shingô-ga-kawa-ru-no-o **ma-ts·u**. [Refer to 4).]

137) I **punched** a time card.

Watashi-wa taimu-kâdo-o **utta**. [Refer to 4).]

138) I **got on** the elevator.

Watashi-wa erebêtâ-ni **notta**. [Refer to 7).]

139) I **changed** clothes in a locker room.

Watashi-wa rokkâ-de ki-**gae-o-shi-ta**. [Refer to 11).]

140) I **took** my seat.

Watashi-wa seki-ni **tsu-i-ta**. [Refer to 1).]

141) We **had** a morning gathering or **had** a pep talk.

Ware-ware-wa chôrei-o **shi-ta**. [Refer to 11).]

142) I **prepared** my material.

Watashi-wa shorui-o **sakusei-shi-ta**. [Refer to 11).]

143) I **wrote** a paper.

Watashi-wa shorui-o **ka-i-ta**. [Refer to 1).]

144) I **submitted** the report.

Watashi-wa hôkoku-sho-o **teishutsu-shi-ta**. [Refer to 11).]

145) I **set up** sale's goal.

Watashi-wa hambai-mokuhyô-o **ta-t·e-ta**. [Refer to 10).]

146) I **read** some documents.

Watashi-wa shorui-o **yo-n-da**. [Refer to 6).]

147) I **stamped** the documents.

Watashi-wa shorui-ni **ôin-shi-ta**. [Refer to 11).]

148) I **wrote up** an account.

Watashi-wa seikyû-sho-o **tsukutta**. [Refer to 7).]

149) I **worked** with the calculator.

Watashi-wa dentaku-de **keisan-shi-ta**. [Refer to 11).]

150) I **typed up** a document on the word processor.

Watashi-wa wâpuro-de bunsho-o **shi-a-g·e-ta**. [Refer to 10).]

151) I **master** word processing.

Watashi-wa wâpuro-o **masutâ-suru**. [Refer to 11).]

152) I **change** Roman letters to Kana syllabary.

Watashi-wa Rôma-ji-o Kana-ni **henkan-suru**. [Refer to 11).]

153) I **file** the material on a floppy disk.

Watashi-wa dêta-o furoppî-disuku-ni **hokan-suru**. [Refer to 11).]

154) I **send** a fax.

Watashi-wa fakkusu-o **oku-r·u**. [Refer to 7).]

155) I **make** some copies.

Watashi-wa kopî-o **to-r·u**. [Refer to 7).]

156) I **make** 3 photocopies of these papers.

Watashi-wa shorui-o san-bu **kopî-suru**. [Refer to 11).]

157) I **set** the copy machine in the enlargement position.

Watashi-wa kopî-ki-o kakudai-ni **setto-suru**. [Refer to 11).]

158) I **reduce** the page to 70%.

Watashi-wa pêji-o nanajuppâsento-ni **shukushô-suru.** [Refer to 11).]

159) I **make** a call.

Watashi-wa denwa-o **ka-k·eru**. [Refer to 10).]

160) I **take** a call.

Watashi-wa denwa-ni **d·eru**. [Refer to 10).]

161) I **hang up** the phone.

Watashi-wa denwa-o **ki-r·u**. [Refer to 7).]

162) I **am called** by my boss.

Watashi-wa jôshi-ni **yoba-r·eru**. [Refer to aux. 1).]

163) I **was scolded** by him.

Watashi-wa kare-ni **shika-rar·e-ta**. [Refer to aux. 2).]

164) I **exchange** business card.

Watashi-wa meishi-o **kôkan-suru**. [Refer to 11).]

165) I **feel** the stress.

Watashi-wa sutoresu-ga **tama-r·u**. [Refer to 7).]

166) I **go** into the dining room.

Watashi-wa shokudô-e **i-k·u**. [Refer to 1).]

167) I **attend** the meeting.

Watashi-wa kaigi-ni **shusseki-suru**. [Refer to 11).]

168) The meeting **lasted** till late.

Kaigi-wa oso-ku-made **tsuzu-i-ta**. [Refer to 1).]

169) I **stepped out** the meeting for a while.

Watashi-wa shibaraku seki-o **hazu-sh·i-ta**. [Refer to 3).]

170) I often **do** business outside the company.

Watashi-wa yoku eigyô-de soto-mawari-o **suru**. [Refer to 11).]

171) At last I **fulfilled** the goal.

Watashi-wa yatto noruma-o **tassei-shi-ta**. [Refer to 11).]

172) I **work overtime** from 5 to 8.

Watashi-wa go-ji-kara hachi-ji-made **zangyô-suru**. [Refer to 11).]

173) I **change back** to street clothes.

Watashi-wa shifuku-ni **ki-ga-eru**. [Refer to 10).].

174) I **go home**.

Watashi-wa **taisha-suru**. [Refer to 11).]

175) I **stand and read** in a bookstore.

Watashi-wa shoten-de **tachi-yomi-suru**. [Refer to 11).]

176) I **meet** someone at a ticket gate (of the station).

Watashi-wa (eki-no) kaisatsu-guchi-de hito-to **machi-awase-o-suru**. [Refer to 11).]

177) I **go out** for dinner with a friend.

Watashi-wa tomodachi-to yûshoku-ni **i-k·u**. [Refer to 1).]

178) I **take** a guest **out** to dinner.

Watashi-wa o-kyaku-o yûshoku-ni **tsure-da-s·u**. [Refer to 3).]

179) I **go out** for drink.

Watashi-wa nomi-ni **i-k·u**. [Refer to 1).]

180) I **reserve** a bottle (of whisk(e)y).

Watashi-wa (uisukî no) botoru-o **kîpu-<u>suru</u>**. [Refer to 11).]

181) I **wipe** my face with hot towel.

Watashi-wa atsu-i taoru-de kao-o **fu-k·u**. [Refer to 1).]

182) I **catch** a taxi.

Watashi-wa takushî-o **hiro-u**. [Refer to 8).]

183) I **drive** a car.

Watashi-wa kuruma-o **unten-<u>suru</u>**. [Refer to 11).]

184) I **drive** safely.

Watashi-wa **anzen-unten-o-<u>suru</u>**. [Refer to 11).]

185) I **start** the engine.

Watashi-wa enjin-o **ka-k·eru**. [Refer to 10).]

186) I **fasten** the seatbelt.

Watashi-wa shîtoberuto-o **shi-m·eru**. [Refer to 10).]

187) I **release** an emergency brake.

Watashi-wa saido-burêki-o **oro-s·u**. [Refer to 3).]

188) I **shift** gears.

Watashi-wa gia-o **ka-k·eru**. [Refer to 10).]

189) I **get** a car *out of* the garage.

Watashi-wa garêji-kara kuruma-o **da-s·u**. [Refer to 3).]

190) I **wait** for a light.

Watashi-wa shingô-o **ma-ts·u**. [Refer to 4).]

191) I **speed up**.

Watashi-wa **zôsoku-suru**. [Refer to 11).]

192) I **put on** the brakes.

Watashi-wa burêki-o **ka-k·eru**. [Refer to 10).]

193) I **turn right**.

Watashi-wa **usetsu-suru**. [Refer to 11).]

194) I **turn left**.

Watashi-wa **sasetsu-suru**. [Refer to 11).]

195) I **change** line.

Watashi-wa shasen-o **henkô-suru**. [Refer to 11).]

196) I **get over** to the left lane.

Watashi-wa hidari-shasen-ni **utsu-r·u**. [Refer to 7).]

197) I **pay** a toll at the toll gate.

Watashi-wa ryôkin-sho-de tsûkô-ryô-o **hara-u**. [Refer to 8).]

198) I **wash** my car.

Watashi-wa kuruma-o **ara-u**. [Refer to 8).]

199) I **leave** the car in a parking lot.

Watashi-wa chûsha-jô-ni kuruma-o **to-m·eru**. [Refer to 10).]

200) I **stop** the engine.

Watashi-wa enjin-o **to-m·eru**. [Refer to 10).]

201) I **load** my baggage in the car.

Watashi-wa kuruma-ni nimotsu-o **tsu-m·u**. [Refer to 6).]

202) I **locked** my car with the key inside.

Watashi-wa kuruma-no-naka-ni kî-o-oita-mama **rokku-shi-ta**. [Refer to 11).]

203) I **left** the dome light **on**.

Watashi-wa shitsunai-tô-o **tsukeppanashi-ni-shi-ta**. [Refer to 11).]

204) I **forgot** to turn off the lights.

Watashi-wa raito-o keshi-**wasu-r·e-ta**. [Refer to

10).]

205) I **had my license suspended** for 30 days for speeding.

Watashi-wa supîdo-ihan-de sanjû-nichi **mentei-ni-sa-r·e-ta**. [Refer to aux. 1).]

206) He **had** a head-on collision.

Kare-wa shômen-shôtotsu-o **shi-ta**. [Refer to 11).]

207) He **caused** a traffic accident resulting in injury.

Kare-wa jinshin-jiko-o **oko-sh·i-ta**. [Refer to 3).]

208) He **drove** a car half asleep.

Kare-wa inemuri-**unten-o-shi-ta**. [Refer to 11).]

209) I **called** Japan Automobile Foundation for help.

Watashi-wa JAF-ni tasuke-o **motom·e-ta**. [Refer to 10).]

210) I **open** an account.

Watashi-wa kôza-o **kaisetsu-suru**. [Refer to 11).]

211) I **withdraw** some money from the bank.

Watashi-wa ginkô-kara kane-o **oro-s·u**. [Refer to 3).]

212) I **withdraw** some money with the bank card.

Watashi-wa kâdo-de kane-o **oro-s·u**. [Refer to 3).]

213) I **deposit** ¥100,000.

Watashi-wa jûman-en-o **azu-k·eru**. [Refer to 10).]

214) I **pay** charges for public services at the bank.

Watashi-wa ginkô-de kôkyô-ryôkin-o **hara-u**. [Refer to 8).]

215) I **cash** the check.

Watashi-wa ko-gitte-o **genkin-ni-ka-eru**. [Refer to 10).]

216) I **deposit** the check in a bank.

Watashi-wa ginkô-ni ko-gitte-o **azu-k·eru**. [Refer to 10).]

217) I **discount** the bill.

Watashi-wa tegata-o **wa-r·u**. [Refer to 7).]

218) I **put** 500,000 yen into a fixed deposit account.

Watashi-wa gojûman-en-o teiki-yokin-ni **i-r·eru**. [Refer to 10).]

219) I **request** today's rate.

Watashi-wa kyô-no rêto-o **tazu-n·eru**. [Refer to 10).]

Here, paying attention to Grammar, we will give tables of conjugation of verbs and auxiliaries. To get a better understanding of conjugation, we will separate stems (which do not conjugate) and conjugating parts; consequently hyphens and centered periods are used frequently. Since overuse of hyphens, however, may become an obstacle for smooth reading, their use is not adopted in and after Part II.

ex.	ma-su	masu
	na-i	nai
	i-k·u	iku

In the syllabification, we do not put a hypen in case of geminated consonants or lengthened vowels, since it is impossible to separate stems and endings.

ex.	nakatta	na-kat-ta
	ma-shô	ma-sho-u
	itte	it-te
	itta	it-ta

The italicized expression in parentheses is a polite expression. Personal pronouns in parentheses can be omitted freely.

The table of conjugation of verbs

1) **to write (ka-k·u)**
   *to go (i-k·u)
   to brush (miga-k·u)
   to bake (ya-k·u) etc.

   (k·u in the k series of the Kana syllabary conjugates as follows:)

   I **write** a letter.
   Watashi-wa tegami-o **ka-k·u**(*ka-k·i-ma-su*).
   I **don't write** a letter.
   Watashi-wa tegami-o **ka-k·a-na-i**(*ka-k·i-ma-se-n*).
   I **can write** a letter.
   Watashi-wa tegami-o **ka-k·u-koto-ga-deki-ru** = **ka-k·e-ru**(*ka-k·u-koto-ga-deki-ma-su* = *ka-k·e-ma-su*).
   I **am writing** a letter.
   Watashi-wa tegami-o **ka-i-te-i-ru**(*ka-i-te-i-ma-su*).
   I **write** a letter **and** . . .
   Watashi-wa tegami-o **ka-k·i** or **ka-i-te** . . .
   *I **go** to Tom's house **and** . . .
   Watashi-wa Tomu-no ie-e **i-k·i** or **itte** . . .
   If I **write** a letter, . . .
   (Watashi-wa) Tegami-o **ka-k·e-ba**, . . .

If I **don't write** a letter, . . .

(Watashi-wa) Tegami-o **ka-k·a-na-ke-re-ba**, . . .

Write a letter.

Tegami-o **ka-k·e**(*ka-k·i-nasa-i*).

Don't write a letter.

Tegami-o **ka-k·u-na**(*ka-k·i-nasa-n-na*).

Let's write letters.

Tegami-o **ka-k·ô**(*ka-k·i-ma-shô*).

I **wrote** a letter.

Watashi-wa tegami-o **ka-i-ta**(*ka-k·i-ma-shi-ta*).

*I **went** there.

Watashi-wa soko-e **itta**(*i-k·i-ma-shi-ta*).

I **didn't write** a letter.

Watashi-wa tegami-o **ka-k·a-na-katta**(*ka-k·i-ma-se-n-de-shi-ta*).

I'll **write** a letter.

Watashi-wa tegami-o **ka-k·u-da-rô**(*ka-k·u-de-shô*).

I'll **not write** a letter.

Watashi-wa tegami-o **ka-k·a-na-i-da-rô**(*ka-k·a-na-i-de-shô*).

2) **to swim (oyo-g·u)**
to rinse (susu-g·u)
to take off (nu-g·u) etc.

(g·u in the g series of the Kana syllabary conjugates as follows:)

I swim.

Watashi-wa **oyo-g·u**(*oyo-g·i-ma-su*).

I don't swim.

Watashi-wa **oyo-g·a-na-i**(*oyo-g·i-ma-se-n*).

I can swim.

Watashi-wa **oyo-g·u-koto-ga-deki-ru** = **oyo-g·e-ru** (*oyo-g·u-koto-ga-deki-ma-su* = *oyo-g·e-ma-su*).

I am swimming.

Watashi-wa **oyo-i-de-i-ru**(*oyo-i-de-i-ma-su*).

I swim and . . .

Watashi-wa **oyo-g·i** or **oyo-i-de** . . .

If I swim, . . .

(Watashi-wa) **Oyo-g·e-ba**, . . .

If I don't swim, . . .

(Watashi-wa) **Oyo-g·a-na-ke-re-ba**, . . .

Swim.

Oyo-g·e(*Oyo-g·i-nasa-i*).

Don't swim.

Oyo-g·u-na(*Oyo-g·i-nasa-n-na*).

Let's swim.

Oyo-g·ô(*Oyo-g·i-ma-shô*).

I **swam**.

Watashi-wa **oyo-i-da**(*oyo-g·i-ma-shi-ta*).

I **didn't swim**.

Watashi-wa **oyo-g·a-na-katta** (*oyo-g·i-ma-se-n-de-shi-ta*).

I'**ll swim** this afternoon.

Watashi-wa kyô-gogo **oyo-g·u-da-rô**(*oyo-g·u-de-shô*).

I'll not swim this afternoon.

Watashi-wa kyô-gogo **oyo-g·a-na-i-da-rô** (*oyo-g·a-na-i-de-shô*).

3) **to switch off (ke-s·u)**
to boil (waka-s·u)
to unload (oro-s·u)
to dry (kawaka-s·u) etc.

(s·u in the s series of the Kana syllabary conjugates as follows:)

I **switch off** the light.
Watashi-wa denki-o **ke-s·u** (*ke-sh·i-ma-su*).
I **don't switch off** the light.
Watashi-wa denki-o **ke-s·a-na-i**(*ke-sh·i-ma-se-n*).
I **can switch off** the light.
Watashi-wa denki-o **ke-s·u-koto-ga-deki-ru = ke-s·e-ru** (*ke-s·u-koto-ga-deki-ma-su = ke-s·e-ma-su*).
I **am switching off** the light now.
Watashi-wa ima denki-o **ke-sh·i-te-i-ru**(*ke-sh·i-te-i-ma-su*).
I **switch off** the light **and** . . .
Watashi-wa denki-o **ke-sh·i** or **ke-sh·i-te** . . .
If I **switch off** the light, . . .
(Watashi-wa) Denki-o **ke-s·e-ba**, . . .
If I **don't switch off** the light, . . .
(Watashi-wa) Denki-o **ke-s·a-na-ke-re-ba**, . . .
Switch off the light.

Denki-o **ke-s·e**(*ke-sh·i-nasa-i*).

Don't switch off the light.

Denki-o **ke-s·u-na**(*ke-sh·i-nasa-n-na*).

Let's switch off the light.

Denki-o **ke-s·ô**(*ke-sh·i-ma-shô*).

I **switched off** the light.

Watashi-wa denki-o **ke-sh·i-ta**(*ke-sh·i-ma-shi-ta*).

I **didn't switch off** the light.

Watashi-wa denki-o **ke-s·a-na-katta**(*ke-sh·i-ma-se-n-de-shi-ta*).

I'll switch off the light.

Watashi-wa denki-o **ke-s·u-da-rô**(*ke-s·u-de-shô*).

I'll not switch off the light.

Watashi-wa denki-o **ke-s·a-na-i-da-rô**(*ke-s·a-na-i-de-shô*).

4) **to wait (ma-ts·u)**
to stand (up) (ta-ts·u) etc.

(ts·u in the t series of the Kana syllabary conjugates as follows:)

I **wait** for him.

Watashi-wa kare-o **ma-ts·u**(*ma-ch·i-ma-su*).

I **don't wait** for him.

Watashi-wa kare-o **ma-t·a-na-i**(*ma-ch·i-ma-se-n*).

I **can wait** for him.

Watashi-wa kare-o **ma-ts·u-koto-ga-deki-ru = ma-t·e ru**(*ma-ts·u-koto-ga-deki-ma-su = ma-t·e-ma-su*).

I **am waiting** for him.

Watashi-wa kare-o **matte-i-ru**(*matte-i-ma-su*).

I **wait** for him and . . .

Watashi-wa kare-o **ma-ch·i** or **matte** . . .

If I **wait** for her, . . .

(Watashi-wa) Kano-jo-o **ma-t·e-ba**, . . .

If I **don't wait** for her, . . .

(Watashi-wa) Kano-jo-o **ma-t·a-na-ke-re-ba**, . . .

Wait for her.

Kano-jo-o **ma-t·e**(*ma-ch·i-nasa-i*).

Don't wait for her.

Kano-jo-o **ma-ts·u-na**(*ma-ch·i-nasa-n-na*).

Let's wait for her.

Kano-jo-o **ma-t·ô**(*ma-ch·i-ma-shô*).

I **waited** for her.

Watashi-wa kano-jo-o matta(*ma-ch·i-ma-shi-ta*).

I didn't wait for her.

Watashi-wa kano-jo-o **ma-t·a-na-katta**(*ma-ch·i-ma-se-n-de-shi-ta*).

I'll **wait** for her.

Watashi-wa kano-jo-o **ma-ts·u-da-rô**(*ma-ts·u-de-shô*).

I'll **not wait** for her.

Watashi-wa kano-jo-o **ma-t·a-na-i-da-rô**(*ma-t·a-na-i-de-shô*).

5) **to choose (era-b·u)**
to line up (nara-b·u)
to fly (to-b·u) etc.

(b·u in the b series of the Kana syllabary conjugates as follows:)

I **choose** a present for her.

Watashi-wa kano-jo-ni okurimono-o **era-b·u**(*era-b·i-ma-su*).

I **don't choose** a present for her.

Watashi-wa kano-jo-ni okurimono-o **era-b·a-na-i**(*era-b·i-ma-se-n*).

I **can choose** whatever I like.

Watashi-wa dore-demo su-ki-na mono-o **era-b·u-koto-ga-deki-ru = era-b·e-ru**(*era-b·u-koto-ga-deki-ma-su = era-b·e-ma-su*).

I **am choosing** a present for her.

Watashi-wa kano-jo-ni okurimono-o **era-n̲-de-i-ru**(*era-n̲-de-i-ma-su*).

I **choose** a present for her **and** . . .

Watashi-wa kano-jo-ni okurimono-o **era-b·i** or **era-n̲-de** . . .

If I **choose** a present for her, . . .

(Watashi-wa) Kano-jo-ni okurimono-o **era-b·e-ba**, . . .

If I **don't choose** a present for her, . . .

(Watashi-wa) Kano-jo-ni okurimono-o **era-b·a-na-ke-re-ba**, . . .

Choose a present for her.

Kano-jo-ni okurimono-o **era-b·e**(*era-b·i-nasa-i*).

Don't choose anything.

Nani-mo **era-b·u-na**(*era-b·i-nasa-n-na*).

Let's choose a present for her.

Kano-jo-ni okurimono-o **era-b·ô**(*era-b·i-ma-shô*).

I **chose** a present for her.

Watashi-wa kano-jo-ni okurimono-o **era-n-da**(*era-b·i-ma-shi-ta*).

I **didn't choose** anything.

Watashi-wa nani-mo **era-b·a-na-katta**(*era-b·i-ma-se-n-de-shi-ta*).

I'll **choose** a present for her.

Watashi-wa kano-jo-ni okurimono-o **era-b·u-da-rô** (*era-b·u-de-shô*).

I'll **not choose** anything.

Watashi-wa nani-mo **era-b·a-na-i-da-rô**(*era-b·a-na-i-de-shô*).

6) **to read (yo-m·u)**
to chop (kiza-m·u)
to load (tsu-m·u) etc.

(m·u of the m series of the Kana syllabary conjugates as follows:)

I **read** a book.

Watashi-wa hon-o **yo-m·u**(*yo-m·i-ma-su*).

I **don't read** the newspaper.

Watashi-wa shimbun-o **yo-m·a-na-i**(*yo-m·i-ma-se-n*).

I **can read** this book.

Watashi-wa kono hon-o **yo-m·u-koto-ga-deki-ru = yo-m·e-ru**(*yo-m·u-koto-ga-deki-ma-su = yo-m·e-ma-su*).

I **am reading** the newspaper.

Watashi-wa shimbun-o **yo-n̲-de-i-ru**(*yo-n̲-de-i-ma-su*).

I **read** the newspaper **and** . . .

Watashi-wa shimbun-o **yo-m·i** or **yo-n̲-de** . . .

If I **read** the newspaper, . . .

(Watashi-wa) Shimbun-o **yo-m·e-ba**, . . .

If I **don't read** the newspaper, . . .

(Watashi-wa) Shimbun-o **yo-m·a-na-ke-re-ba**, . . .

Read the newspaper.

Shimbun-o **yo-m·e**(*yo-m·i-nasa-i*).

Don't read it.

Sore-o **yo-m·u-na**(*yo-m·i-nasa-n-na*).

Let's read this comic.

Kono manga-o **yo-m·ô**(*yo-m·i-ma-shô*).

I **read** the newspaper this morning.

Watashi-wa kesa shimbun-o **yo-n-da**(*yo-m·i-ma-shi-ta*).

I **didn't read** the newspaper this morning.

Watashi-wa kesa shimbun-o **yo-m·a-na-katta**(*yo-m·i-ma-se-n-de-shi-ta*).

I'll **read** the newspaper.

Watashi-wa shimbun-o **yo-m·u-da-rô**(*yo-m·u-de-shô*).

I'll **not read** the newspaper.

Watashi-wa shimbun-o **yo-m·a-na-i-da-rô**(*yo-m·a-na-i-de-shô*).

7) **to make (tsuku-r·u)**
to send (oku-r·u)
to get on (no-r·u)
to cut (ki-r·u) etc.

(r·u in the r series of the Kana syllabary conjugates as follows:)

I **make** salad.

Watashi-wa sarada-o **tsuku-r·u**(*tsuku-r·i-ma-su*).

I **don't make** salad.

Watashi-wa sarada-o **tsuku-r·a-na-i**(*tsuku-r·i-ma-se-n*).

I **can make** salad.

Watashi-wa sarada-o **tsuku-r·u-koto-ga-deki-ru** = **tsuku-r·e-ru**(*tsuku-r·u-koto-ga-deki-ma-su* = *tsuku-r·e-ma-su*).

I **am making** salad.

Watashi-wa sarada-o **tsukutte-i-ru**(*tsukutte-i-ma-su*).

I **make** salad **and** . . .

Watashi-wa sarada-o **tsuku-r·i** or **tsukutte** . . .

If I **make** salad, . . .

(Watashi-wa) Sarada-o **tsuku-r·e-ba**, . . .

If I **don't make** salad, . . .

(Watashi-wa) Sarada-o **tsuku-r·a-na-ke-re-ba**, . . .

Make salad.

Sarada-o **tsuku-r·e**(*tsuku-r·i-nasa-i*).

Don't make salad this morning.

Kesa sarada-o **tsuku-r·u-na**(*tsuku-r·i-nasa-n-na*).

Let's make salad.

Sarada-o **tsuku-r·ô**(*tsuku-r·i-ma-shô*).

I **made** salad.

Watashi-wa sarada-o **tsukutta**(*tsuku-r·i-ma-shi-ta*).

I **didn't make** salad.

Watashi-wa sarada-o **tsuku-r·a-na-katta**(*tsuku-r·i-ma-se-n-de-shi-ta*).

I'll **make** salad.

Watashi-wa sarada-o **tsuku-r·u-da-rô**(*tsuku-r·u-de-shô*).

I'll **not make** salad tomorrow morning.

Watashi-wa asu-asa sarada-o **tsuku-r·a-na-i-da-rô** (*tsuku-r·a-na-i-de-shô*).

8) **to wash (ara-u)**
to buy (ka-u)
to sing (uta-u)
to pay (hara-u) etc.

(u in the w series of the Kana syllabary conjugates as follows:)

I **wash** them.

Watashi-wa sore-ra-o **ara-u**(*ara-i-ma-su*).

I **don't wash** them.

Watashi-wa sore-ra-o **ara-w·a-na-i**(*ara-i-ma-se-n*).

I **can wash** them.

Watashi-wa sore-ra-o **ara-u-koto-ga-deki-ru** = **ara-e-ru** (*ara-u-koto-ga-deki-ma-su* = *ara-e-ma-su*).

I **am washing** them.

Watashi-wa sore-ra-o **aratte-i-ru**(*aratte-i-ma-su*).

I **wash** them **and** . . .

Watashi-wa sore-ra-o **ara-i** or **aratte** . . .

If I **wash** them, . . .

(Watashi-wa) Sore-ra-o **ara-e-ba**, . . .

If I **don't wash** them, . . .

(Watashi-wa) Sore-ra-o **ara-w·a-na-ke-re-ba**, . . .

Wash them.

Sore-ra-o **ara-e**(*ara-i-nasa-i*).

Don't wash them now.

Ima sore-ra-o **ara-u-na**(*ara-i-nasa-n-na*).

Let's wash them.

Sore-ra-o **ara-ô**(*ara-i-ma-shô*).

I **washed** them.

Watashi-wa sore-ra-o **aratta**(*ara-i-ma-shi-ta*).

I **didn't wash** them.

Watashi-wa sore-ra-o **ara-w·a-na-katta**(*ara-i-ma-se-n-de-shi-ta*).

I'll **wash** them.

Watashi-wa sore-ra-o **ara-u-da-rô**(*ara-u-de-shô*).

I'll **not wash** them.

Watashi-wa sore-ra-o **ara-w·a-na-i-da-rô**(*ara-w·a-na-i-de-shô*).

(i)

9) **to boil (n·iru)**
to put on (k·iru)
to see (m·iru)
to get off (o-r·iru) etc.

(-ru after i conjugates as follows:)

I **boil** potatoes.
Watashi-wa jagaimo-o **n·iru**(*n·i-ma-su*).
I **don't boil** potatoes.
Watashi-wa jagaimo-o **n·i-na-i**(*n·i-ma-se-n*).
I **am boiling** potatoes.
Watashi-wa jagaimo-o **n·i-te-i-ru**(*n·i-te-i-ma-su*).
I **boil** potatoes **and** . . .
Watashi-wa jagaimo-o **n·i** or **n·i-te** . . .
If I **boil** potatoes, . . .
(Watashi-wa) Jagaimo-o **n·ire-ba**, . . .
If I **don't boil** potatoes, . . .
(Watashi-wa) Jagaimo-o **n·i-na-ke-re-ba**, . . .
Boil potatoes.
Jagaimo-o **n·iro**(*n·i-nasa-i*).
Don't boil potatoes.
Jagaimo-o **n·iru-na**(*n·i-nasa-n-na*).

Let's boil potatoes.

Jagaimo-o **n·iyô**(*n·i-ma-shô*).

I **boiled** potatoes.

Watashi-wa jagaimo-o **n·i-ta**(*n·i-ma-shi-ta*).

I **didn't boil** potatoes.

Watashi-wa jagaimo-o **n·i-na-katta**(*n·i-ma-se-n-de-shi-ta*).

I'll **boil** potatoes.

Watashi-wa jagaimo-o **n·iru-da-rô**(*n·iru-de-shô*).

I'll **not boil** potatoes.

Watashi-wa jagaimo-o **n·i-na-i-da-rô**(*n·i-na-i-de-shô*).

(e)

10) **to open (a-k·eru)**
to give (ata-eru)
to fry (a-g·eru)
to eat (ta-b·eru)
to put (i-r·eru)

(-ru after e conjugates as follows:)

I **open** the windows.
Watashi-wa mado-o **a-k·eru**(*a-k·e-ma-su*).
I **don't open** the windows.
Watashi-wa mado-o **a-k·e-na-i**(*a-k·e-ma-se-n*).
I **am opening** the windows.
Watashi-wa mado-o **a-k·e-te-i-ru**(*a-k·e-te-i-ma-su*).
I **open** the windows **and** . . .
Watashi-wa mado-o **a-k·e** or **a-k·e-te** . . .
If I **open** the windows, . . .
(Watashi-wa) Mado-o **a-k·ere-ba**, . . .
If I **don't open** the windows, . . .
(Watashi-wa) Mado-o **a-k·e-na-ke-re-ba**, . . .
Open the windows.
Mado-o **a-k·ero** (*a-k·e-nasa-i*).
Don't open the windows.

Mado-o **a-k·eru-na**(*a-k·e-nasa-n-na*).

Let's open the windows.

Mado-o **a-k·eyô**(*a-k·e-ma-shô*).

I **opene**d the windows.

Watashi-wa mado-o **a-k·e-ta**(*a-k·e-ma-shi-ta*).

I **didn't open** the windows.

Watashi-wa mado-o **a-k·e-na-katta**(*a-k·e-ma-se-n-de-shi-ta*).

I'**ll open** the windows.

Watashi-wa mado-o **a-k·eru-da-rô**(*a-k·eru-de-shô*).

I'**ll not open** the windows.

Watashi-wa mado-o **a-k·e-nai-da-rô**(*a-k·e-nai-de-shô*).

11) **to do (suru); **to submit (teishutsu-suru)**

(**suru** or **-suru** and **kuru** (to come 12)) conjugate irregularly.)

I **do** it.

Watashi-wa sore-o **suru**(*shi-ma-su*).

I **submit the report.

Watashi-wa hôkoku-sho-o **teishutsu-suru**(*teishutsu-shi-ma-su*).

I **don't do** it.

Watashi-wa sore-o **shi-na-i**(*shi-ma-se-n*).

I **don't submit the report.

Watashi-wa hôkoku-sho-o **teishutsu-shi-na-i** (*teishutsu-shi-ma-se-n*).

I **can do** it.

Watashi-wa sore-o **suru-koto-ga-deki-ru**(*suru-koto-ga-deki-ma-su*).

I **can submit the report.

Watashi-wa hôkoku-sho-o **teishutsu-suru-koto-ga-deki-ru**(*teishutsu-suru-koto-ga-deki-ma-su*).

I **am doing** it.

Watashi-wa sore-o **shi-te-i-ru**(*shi-te-i-ma-su*).

I **am submitting the report.

Watashi-wa hôkoku-sho-o **teishutsu-shi-te-i-ru**(*teishutsu-shi-te-i-ma-su*).

I **do** it **and** . . .

Watashi-wa sore-o **shi** or **shi-te** . . .

I **submit the report **and** . . .

Watashi-wa hôkoku-sho-o **teishutsu-shi** or **teishutsu-shi-te** . . .

If I **do** it, . . .

(Watashi-wa) Sore-o **sure-ba**, . . .

****If** I **submit** the report, . . .

(Watashi-wa) Hôkoku-sho-o **teishutsu-sure-ba**, . . .

If I **don't do** it, . . .

(Watashi-wa) Sore-o **shi-na-ke-re-ba**, . . .

****If** I **don't submit** the report, . . .

(Watashi-wa) Hôkoku-sho-o **teishutsu-shi-na-ke-re-ba**, . . .

Do it.

Sore-o **seyo**(*shi-nasa-i*).

****Submit** the report.

Hôkoku-sho-o **teishutsu-shi-ro**(*teishutsu-shi-nasa-i*).

Don't do it.

Sore-o **suru-na**(*shi-nasa-n-na*).

****Don't submit** the report.

Hôkoku-sho-o **teishutsu-suru-na**(*teishutsu-shi-nasa-n-na*).

Let's do it.

Sore-o **shiyô**(*shi-ma-shô*).

Let's submit the reports.

Hôkoku-sho-o **teishutsu-shiyô**(*teishutsu-shi-ma-shô*).

I **did** it.

Watashi-wa sore-o **shi-ta**(*shi-ma-shi-ta*).

I **submitted the report.

Watashi-wa hôkoku-sho-o **teishutsu-shi-ta**(*teishutsu-shi-ma-shi-ta*).

I **didn't do** it.

Watashi-wa sore-o **shi-na-katta**(*shi-ma-se-n-de-shi-ta*).

I **didn't submit the report.

Watashi-wa hôkoku-sho-o **teishutsu-shi-na-katta** (*teishutsu-shi-ma-se-n-de-shi-ta*).

I'll **do** it.

Watashi-wa sore-o **suru-da-rô**(*suru-de-shô*).

I'll **submit the report.

Watashi-wa hôkoku-sho-o **teishutsu-suru-da-rô** (*teishutsu-suru-de-shô*).

I'll **not do** it.

Watashi-wa sore-o **shi-na-i-da-rô**(*shi-na-i-de-shô*).

I'll **not submit the report.

Watashi-wa hôkoku-sho-o **teishutsu-shi-na-i-da-rô** (*teishutsu-shi-na-i-de-shô*).

12) **to come (kuru)**

He **comes** to Tokyo.

Kare-wa Tôkyô-ni **kuru**(*ki-ma-su*).

She **doesn't come** to Tokyo.

Kano-jo-wa Tôkyô-ni **ko-nai**(*ki-ma-se-n*).

A friend **comes** to Osaka **and** . . .

Tomodachi-ga Ôsaka-ni **ki** or **ki-te** . . .

If John **comes** to Nagoya, . . .

Jon-ga Nagoya-ni **kure-ba**, . . .

If Jane **doesn't come** to Nagoya, . . .

Jên-ga Nagoya-ni **ko-na-kere-ba**, . . .

Come to Kobe.

Kôbe-ni **koi**(*ki-nasa-i*).

Don't come here.

Koko-e **kuru-na**(*ki-nasa-n-na*).

Let's come to Kobe next time.

Kondo Kôbe-ni **koyô**(*ki-ma-shô*).

Yesterday John **came** to Kobe.

Kinô Jon-wa Kôbe-ni **ki-ta**(*ki-ma-shi-ta*).

Jane **didn't come** to Kobe after all.

Jên-wa tôtô Kôbe-ni **ko-nakatta**(*ki-ma-se-n-de-shi-ta*).

John **will come** to Okayama tomorrow.

Asu Jon-wa Okayama-ni **kuru-da-rô**(*kuru-de-shô*).

Jane **will not come** to Nagasaki tomorrow.

Asu Jên-wa Nagasaki-ni **ko-na-i-da-rô**(*ko-na-i-de-shô*).

The table of conjugation of auxiliaries

1) **to be called (yoba-r·eru)**
(·eru after r conjugates as follows:)

I **am called** by my mother.
Watashi-wa haha-ni **yoba-r·eru**(*yoba-r·e-ma-su*).

I **am not called** by my mother.
Watashi-wa haha-ni **yoba-r·e-na-i**(*yoba-r·e-ma-se-n*).

I **am called** by my mother **and** . . .
Watashi-wa haha-ni **yoba-r·e-te** . . .

If I **am called** by my mother, . . .
(Watashi-wa) Haha-ni **yoba-r·ere-ba**, . . .

If I **am not called** by my mother, . . .
(Watashi-wa) Haha-ni **yoba-r·e-na-ke-re-ba**, . . .

I **was called** by my mother.
Watashi-wa haha-ni **yoba-r·e-ta**(*yoba-r·e-ma-shi-ta*).

I **was not called** by my mother.
Watashi-wa haha-ni **yoba-r·e-na-katta**(*yoba-r·e-ma-se-n-de-shi-ta*).

I'**ll be called** by my mother.
Watashi-wa haha-ni **yoba-r·eru-da-rô**(*yoba-r·eru-de-shô*).

I'**ll not be called** by my mother.

Watashi-wa haha-ni **yoba-r·e-na-i-da-rô**(*yoba-r·e-na-i-de-shô*).

2) **to be scolded (shika-rar·eru); to be drilled (shibo-rar·eru)**

(·eru after rar conjugates as follows:)

I **am scolded** by my mother.

Watashi-wa haha-ni **shika-rar·eru**(*shika-rar·e-ma-su*).

I **am not scolded** by my mother.

Watashi-wa haha-ni **shika-rar·e-na-i**(*shika-rar·e-ma-se-n*).

I **am scolded** by my mother **and** . . .

Watashi-wa haha-ni **shika-rar·e** or **shika-rar·e-te** . . .

If I **am scolded** by my mother, . . .

(Watashi-wa) Haha-ni **shika-rar·ere-ba**, . . .

If I **am not scolded** by my mother, . . .

(Watashi-wa) Haha-ni **shika-rar·e-na-ke-re-ba**, . . .

Get a good **scolding**.

Un-to **shika-rar·ero**(*shika-rar·e-nasa-i*).

Let's be drilled as members of the tennis club.

Tenisu-no kurabu-de **shibo-rar·eyô**(*shibo-rar·e-ma-shô*).

I **was scolded** by my mother.

Watashi-wa haha-ni **shika-rar·e-ta**(*shika-rar·e-ma-shi-ta*).

I **was not scolded** by my mother.

Watashi-wa haha-ni **shika-rar·e-na-katta**(*shika-rar·e-ma-se-n-de-shi-ta*).

I'll **be scolded** by my mother.

Watashi-wa haha-ni **shika-rar·eru-da-rô**(*shika-rar·eru-de-shô*).

I'll **not be scolded** by my mother.

Watashi-wa haha-ni **shika-rar·e-na-i-da-rô**(*shika-rar·e-na-i-de-shô*).

The following are auxiliary verbs which do not appear in the example sentences.

3) **to make (-s·eru)**

(·eru after s conjugates as follows:)

I **make** him read a book.

Watashi-wa kare-ni hon-o yo-ma-**s·eru**(*yo-ma-s·e-ma-su*).

I **don't make** him read a book.

Watashi-wa kare-ni hon-o yo-ma-**s·e-na-i**(*yo-ma-s·e-ma-se-n*).

I **make** him read a book **and** . . .

Watashi-wa kare-ni hon-o yo-ma-**s·e-te** . . .

If I **make** him read a book, . . .

(Watashi-wa) Kare-ni hon-o yo-**ma-s·ere-ba**, . . .

If I **don't make** him read a book, . . .

(Watashi-wa) Kare-ni hon-o yo-ma-**s·e-na-ke-re-ba**, . . .

Make him read a book.

Kare-ni hon-o yo-ma-**s·ero**(*yo-ma-s·e-nasa-i*).

Don't make him read a book.

Kare-ni hon-o yo-ma-**s·eru-na**(*yo-ma-s·e-nasa-n-na*).

Let's make him read a book

Kare-ni hon-o yo-ma-**s·eyô**(*yo-ma-s·e-ma-shô*).

I **made** him read a book.

Watashi-wa kare-ni hon-o yo-ma-**s·e-ta**(*yo-ma-s·e-ma-shi-ta*).

I **didn't make** him read a book.

Watashi-wa kare-ni hon-o yo-ma-**s·e-na-katta**(*yo-ma-s·e-ma-se-n-de-shi-ta*).

I'**ll make** him read a book.

Watashi-wa kare-ni hon-o **yo-ma-s·eru-da-rô**(*yo-ma-s·eru-de-shô*).

I'**ll not make** him read a book.

Watashi-wa kare-ni hon-o yo-ma-**s·e-na-i-da-rô**(*yo-ma-s·e-na-i-de-shô*).

4) **to want (-tai)**

(i of -tai conjugates as follows:)

I **want** to write.
Watashi-wa ka-ki-**tai**.
I **don't want** to write.
Watashi-wa ka-ki-**taku-na-i**.
If you **want** to write, . . .
Anata-ga ka-ki-**takere-ba**, . . .
When you **want** to write, . . .
Anata-ga ka-ki-**tai-toki-ni**, . . .
I **wanted** to write.
Watashi-wa ka-ki-**takatta**.

5) **to be (-da) → (-de-su)**

(-de-su is the polite expression of -da.)

It'**s** a church.

Are-wa kyôkai-**da**(kyôkai-**de-su**).

It'**s not** a church.

Are-wa kyôkai-**de-wa-na-i**(kyôkai-**de-wa-a-ri-ma-se-n**).

If it'**s** a church, . . .

Are-ga kyôkai-**nara**, . . .

It **was** a church.

Are-wa kyôkai-**datta**(kyôkai-**de-shi-ta**).

It'**ll be** a church.

Are-wa kyôkai-**da-rô**(kyôkai-**de-shô**).

6) **-masu**

I **climb** a mountain.

Watashi-wa yama-ni nobo-ri-**masu**. → nobo-**ru**

I **don't climb** a mountain.

Watashi-wa yama-ni nobo-ri-**mase-n**. → nobo-ra-**na-i**

I **climbed** a mountain.

Watashi-wa yama-ni nobo-ri-**mashi-ta**. → nobotta

Daily conversation

1) Time (Jikan)

What time is it now?

Ima **nan-ji**-desu-ka.

It's two. Ni-ji-desu.

It's *about* three. San-ji-*goro*-desu.

It's four *past* five.

Go-ji yompun(-*sugi*)-desu.

It's six *to* seven.

Shichi-ji roppun-*mae*-desu.

It's eight fifteen.

Hachi-ji jû-go-fun-desu.

It's ten forty-five.

Jû-ji-yonjû-go-fun-desu.

Jû-ichi-ji jû-go-fun-mae-desu.

It's noon. Shôgo-desu.

What's *today*? *Kyô-wa* **nan-yôbi**-desu-ka.

It's Wednesday. Suiyô-bi-desu.

What's **the date** today?

Kyô-wa **nan-nichi**-desu-ka.

It's the 5th.　Itsu-ka-desu.

What's your birthday?

Anata-no tanjô-bi-wa **itsu**-desu-ka.

It's June the 16th.

Rokugatsu jû-roku-nichi-desu.

It takes one and a half hours *to* my office.

Watashi-no jimu-sho-*e-wa* ichi-jikan-han kakari-masu.

How long does it take for the Shinkansen to travel *from* Tokyo *to* Osaka?

Shinkansen-de Tôkyô-*kara* Ôsaka-*made* (iku-no-ni) **dore-kurai** kakari-masu-ka.

It takes *over* 3 hours.

San-jikan-*chotto* kakari-masu.

Which train **are** you **going to** take?

Dono ressha-ni noru-**tsumori-desu**-ka.

The one that leaves *at* 3:46 *for* Tokyo.

San-ji yonjû-roppun-*hatsu-no* Tôkyô-*iki*(-ressha)-ni nori-masu.

What time does the department store open?

Depâto-wa nan-ji-ni aki-masu-ka.

It's open *at* 10 in the morning.

Asa jû-ji-*ni* aki-masu.

When did you arrive *here*?

Itsu *kochira-e* tsuki-mashita-ka.

I arrived here *last night.*

Sakuya kochira-e tsuki-mashita.

2) Climate (Tenkô)

It's fine today. Kyô-wa hare-desu.

It's cloudy. Kumotte-i-masu.

It's getting *a bit* cloudy.

Sukoshi kumotte-**ki-mashita**.

It's rainy. Ame-desu.

It **looks like** it's getting to rain.

Ame-ni nari-**sô-desu**. or Ame-ga furi-**sô-desu**.

It blows *hard.*

Kaze-ga *tsuyoku* fuite-i-masu. or Kaze-ga *tsuyoi*-desu.

The wind has stopped. Kaze-ga yami-mashita.

It's cleared up. Sukkari hare-mashita.

It's sultry. Mushiatsui-desu.

It's *very* hot. *Totemo* atsui(-desu)

It's **become** cold. Samuku **natte-ki-mashita**.

It's snowing. Yuki-ga futte-imasu.

3) A weather forecast (Tenki-yohô)

It's fine now, but it'll be cloudy *in the afternoon*, and it'll rain *at night*.

Ima hare-te-i-masu-ga, *gogo-ni-wa* kumori, *yoru-ni-wa* ame-ni-naru-deshô.

The cold front is going south.

Kanrei-zensen-ga nanka-shite-imasu.

The front of rainy season is moving northward.

Baiu-zensen-ga hokujô-shite-imasu.

The chance of the rain *tomorrow* will be 10% *in the morning*, and 30% in the afternoon.

Asu-no kôsui-kakuritsu-wa *gozen-chû-wa* juppâsento, gogo-wa sanjuppâsento-deshô.

The temperature will fall *a little* tomorrow, and it'll be chilly *in the morning and in the evening.*

Asu-wa kion-ga *sukoshi* saga-ri, *asa-yû-wa* hadazamuku naru-deshô.

The air will be very dry on the Pacific side. Be careful *with* fire.

Taihei-yô-gawa-wa kûki-ga taihen kansô-shi-masu. Kaji-*ni* or Hi-no-moto-*ni* go-chûi-kudasai.

Tomorrow's *highest* temperature will be 15°C and the *lowest* 8°C.

Myônichi-no *saikô*-kion-wa jû-go-do, *saitei*-kion-wa hachi-do-deshô.

The typhoon is approaching.

Taifû-ga sekkin-shite-imasu.

The typhoon has hit the Kii Peninsula.

Taifû-ga Kii-hantô-ni jôriku-shi-mashita.

a warning of possible heavy rains and flood
oo-ame-kôzui-keihô

a strong wind and heavy seas warning
kyôfû-harô-keihô

a dry-weather warning kansô-chûi-hô

a snowstorm warning fûsetsu-chûi-hô

4) At the immigration office (Shutsu-nyûgohu-kanri-jimu-sho-de)

May I see your passport?

(Anata-no) Pasupôto-o **misete-kudasai** or **haiken-shi-masu**.

Yes, sir. Hai dôzo.

What's the purpose *of* your trip?

(Anata-no) Ryokô *no* mokuteki-wa **nan**-desu-ka.

Visiting my uncle *in* Kyoto.

Kyôto-*ni-iru* oji-o tazuneru-tame-desu.

How long are you going to stay?

Taizai-kikan-wa dore-kurai-desu-ka.

About 2 months. *Yaku* ni-ka-getsu-desu.

Have a nice trip! Ii go-ryokô-o

5) At the customs (Zeikan-de)

Do you have *anything* to declare?

Shinkoku-suru-mono-ga *nani-ka* ari-masu-ka.

No, I don't. Betsu-ni ari-masen.

What do you have *in* here?

Kono naka-no-mono-wa nan-desu-ka. or Kono *naka-ni-wa* nani-ga haitte-i-masu-ka.

Only a souvenir.

Miyagemono-*dake*-desu.

What's in this bag?

Kono-kaban-ni-wa nani-ga haitte-i-masu-ka.

My clothes and underwear.

Watashi-no ifuku to shitagi-desu.

6) Being greeted (Demukae)

Welcome to Japan, Suzan!

Sûzan, **yôkoso** Nihon-e!

Thank you *very much* for picking me up.

Mukae-ni-ki-te-kudasatte *honto-ni* arigatô.

How long has it been?

Nan-nen-buri-deshô-ka.

Four years, I think.

Yo-nen-buri-da-to omoi-masu.

How was your flight?
Hikô-ki(-no-tabi)-wa **ikaga**-deshita.

Everything went fine. Kaiteki-deshita.

You **must be** tired. Tsukareta-**deshô**.

Oh, no. I'm alive and kicking, as you see.
Iie, chitto-mo. Kono-toori pinpin-shite-i-masu.

Why don't we head *for* our car? Two bags?
Kuruma-*no-hô-e* **mairi-mashô**. Kaban-wa ni-ko.

That's right. Sô-desu.

Let me **take** one. Hitotsu **mochi-mashô**.

7) Self-introduction (Jiko-shôkai)

May I introduce myself?
Jiko-shôkai-shite-**mo-ii-desu-ka**.

My name is John Smith.
Watashi-no namae-wa Jon Sumisu-desu.

I *am from* Boston. Bosuton-*kara ki-mashita.*

Boston is a good place to live in.
Bosuton-wa sumi-yoi-tokoro-desu.

What do you do?

Nani-o nasatte-iru-no-desu-ka.

I'm a student of A University, majoring in political science.

Watashi-wa Ei-daigaku no gakusei-de, seiji-gaku-o senkô-shite-i-masu.

I came here *for* sightseeing.

Watashi-wa kankô-*de* kochira-e ki-mashita.

Mountaineering is my hobby.

Shumi-wa tozan-desu.

When did you arrive here?

Itsu kochira-e tsuki-mashita-ka?

I just arrived here *yesterday* and I'm still suffering from jet lag.

Kinô kochira-e tsuita-bakari-de, jisa-boke-ni komatte-imasu.

8) Introduction (Shôkai)

Mr. Smith, **I'd like** you to meet Mr. Kimura.

Sumisu-san, anata-o Kimura-san-ni go-shôkai-**shimasu**.

Mr. Kimura, this is my friend, Mr. Smith.

Kimura-san, kochira-wa watashi-no yûjin-de Sumisu-san-desu.

How do you do, Mr. Smith.

Hajime-mashite, Sumisu-san.

I'm very glad **to** see you.

O-me-ni-kakare**te**-kôei-desu.

The pleasure is mine. Call me John.

Kochira-koso. Jon-to yonde-kudasai.

9) Visiting someone (Hômon)

May I have your name, please?

Dochira-sama-desu-ka.

My name is John Parker.

(Watashi-no namae-wa) Jon Pâkâ-desu.

I'm glad you could come.

Yôkoso oide-kudasai-mashita.

Thank you very much for inviting me today.

Kyô-wa o-maneki-ni-azukari arigatô-gozai-masu.

I'm afraid you **must take off** your shoes.

(Anata-no) Kutsu-o **nuide-itadaka-nakereba-nari-masen**.

Oh, that's no trouble.

A, kamai-masen.

People from foreign countries usually find it very inconvenient to take off their shoes in the entrance *before* stepping into the floor.

(Yuka-ni) Agaru-*mae-ni* genkan-de kutsu-o nugu-no-wa, gaikoku-kara ko-rareta kata-ni-wa futsû totemo fuben-ni-omo-wareru-deshô.

Well, it was strange *at first*, but I *soon* got used to it.

Sô-desu-ne, *hajime-wa* hen-na-kanji-deshita-ga, *sugu* nare-mashita.

Please come right in.

Dôzo o-hairi-kudasai.

Thank you. Arigatô(-gozai-masu).

Have a seat and make yourself at home.

O-kake-ni-natte o-kutsurogi-kudasai.

Thank you. This is for you.

Arigatô. Kore-o anata-ni-to-omoi-mashite. or Kore-o dôzo.

Oh, you **don't have to do** that.

Ara, sonna koto-o **nasara-naku-temo**.

What a beautiful room! Your yard looks very nice, *too*.

Nan-to kirei-na o-heya-desu-ne! O-niwa-*mo* totemo suteki-desu.

Thank you. **Would you like** some coffee?

Arigatô. Kôhî-wa **ikaga-desu-ka**.

That's great. **Would you mind** if I smoke?

Suteki, yorokonde-itadaki-masu. Tabako-o suttemo-**yoroshii-ka**.

No, please do. **Hai**, dôzo.

How do you like your coffee? With milk *and* sugar?

Kôhî-wa **dono-yô-ni-itashi-mashô**. Miruku *to* satô-wa dô-itashi-mashô.

Black, please. Burakku-de o-negai-shi-masu.

. . . .

Would you like *some more* coffee?

Kôhî-*no-o-kawari*-wa ikaga-desu-ka.

No, thank you. **Ie, mô-kekkô-desu**.

10) Visiting someone at an office (Kaisha-ni hito-o tazuneru)

May I help you?

Donna go-yôken-deshô-ka.

I'**d like** to see Mr. Kato.

Katô-san-ni o-me-ni-kakari-**tai**-no-desu.

I'm sorry he'*s in* a meeting.

Sumi-masen, Katô-wa *tada-ima* kaigi-*chû-desu*.

Do you think he's going to be long?

Nagaku kakari-sô-desu-ka.

I don't think so. Please take a seat and wait *a while*.

Sonna-koto-wa nai-to omoi-masu. O-kake-ni-natte *shibaraku* o-machi-kudasai.

. . . .

Mr. Kimura, I'm very sorry to **have kept you waiting**. The meeting's *over*. Come this way, please.

Kimura-sama, **o-matase-itashi-mashita**. Kaigi-ga *owari*-mashita. Kochira-e dôzo.

11) Leaving one's home (O-itoma)

Oh, it has got so late.

Mô konna-jikan-ni-natte-shimatte.

I was enjoying the conversation **so** much **that** I *completely* lost track of time.

Amari o-hanashi-ga tanoshikatta-no**de** jikan-ga-tatsu-no-o *sukkari* wasurete-i-mashita.

What's the rush?

Sonna-ni o-isogi-ni-nara-naku-temo(-ii-ja-ari-masen-ka).

I've a business appointment at 5.

Go-ji-ni shigoto-no yakusoku-ga ari-masu.

Thank you very much for everything.

(Nani-mo-kamo) Hontô-ni arigatô-gozai-mashita.

. . . .

It was nice of you to show me around.

Achi-kochi misete-itadaki arigatô-gozai-mashita.

I hope you had a nice time.

Yorokonde-itadakete ureshii-desu.

I really don't do anyting.

Nan-no o-kamai-mo deki-mase-zu.

Please give my best regards to your husband **when** he comes home.

Go-shujin-ga o-kaeri-ni-nari-mashita-**ra**, dôzo yoroshiku-o-tsutae-kudasai.

I sure will. Hai, tsutae-masu.

I'**m looking forward to seeing** you in New York *next time*.

Kondo-wa NyûYôku-de (anata-ni) **o-ai-suru-no-o tanoshimi-ni-shite-ori-masu**.

Thank you. Take care.

Arigatô. O-ki-o-tsukete.

12) Hotel reservation (Hoteru-no yoyaku)

I'd like to make a reservation for tomorrow.

Asu-no yoyaku-o shi-tai-no-desu-ga.

A single room *or* a room with twin beds, sir?

Shinguru-desu-ka *sore-tomo* tsuin-desu-ka.

A single room. Shinguru-desu.

I'm afraid *all* the rooms with one bed are booked. **How about** a room with two beds?

Môshi-wake-gozai-masen-ga, shinguru-wa *subete* man-shitsu-ni-natte-ori-masu. Tsuin-de-wa **ikaga-deshô-ka**.

How much is the room? **Ikura**-desu-ka.

16,000 yen, sir.

Ichiman-rokusen-en-de-gozai-masu.

Does that include tax and service charge?

Zei sâbisu-ryô komi-desu-ka.

No, sir. Iie, betsu-ni-natte-ori-masu.

OK. Kekkô-desu. or Wakari-mashita.

May I have your name, sir?

O-namae-o o-kikase-negae-masu-ka.

George Hilton. Jôji Hiruton-desu.

Your phone number, sir?

O-denwa-bangô-wa.

03-3381-4851.

Zero-san, san-san-hachi-ichi, yon-hachi-gô-ichi-desu.

Is that your home number?

(Sore-wa) Go-jitaku-no bangô-desu-ka.

That's correct. Sô-desu.

What time do you think you'*ll be in*?

Nan-ji-ni *go-tôchaku-no-go-yotei-desu*-ka.

By 5:00. Go-ji-*made-ni*(-tsuku-to-omoi-masu).

Thank you, Mr. Hilton.

Arigatô-gozai-mashita, Hiruton-sama.

13) At the hotel (Hoteru-de)

My name is George Hilton. I called from my home.

(Watashi-no namae-wa) Jôji Hiruton-desu. Jitaku-kara denwa-shite-oki-mashita. or denwa-shi-mashita.

Could you please fill in this form with your name, address, phone number, and age?

Kono yôshi-ni (anata-no) o-namae, go-jûsho, o-denwa-bangô, go-nenrei-o go-kinyû-**itadake-masu-ka**.

Here you go. Hai, kore-de.

Mr. Hilton, your room number is 805.

Hiruton-sama, (anata-no) o-heya-bangô-wa hachi-maru-go-de-gozai-masu.

When is your check-out time?

Chekku-auto-wa nan-ji-desu-ka.

At 10 a.m. (Gozen) Jûji-de-gozai-masu.

What are the hours for breakfast?

Chôshoku-no jikan-wa.

You may have it from 7.

Shichi-ji-kara-de-gozai-masu.

Western dishes are served *on* the 2nd floor and Japanese meal *on* the 3rd floor.

Yôshoku-wa ni-kai-*de*, washoku-wa san-gai-*de*-gozai-masu.

The emergency exit is *over there*.

Hijô-guchi-wa *achira-ni*-ari-masu.

Please dial 2 to the front desk.

Furonto-e-wa daiaru-ni-o o-mawashi-kudasai.

14) Asking the way (Michi-o tazuneru)

How to get to Bingo-cho?

Bingo-chô-e-wa **dô-ike-ba-ii-desu-ka**.

Just keep walking for *about* 100 meters.

Hyaku-mêtoru-*hodo* aruite-kudasai.

Where is the post office?

Yûbin-kyoku-wa **doko-ni**-ari-masu-ka.

Make right at that light **and** go straight for about 50 meters.

Ano shingô-o **migi-e magatte** gojû-mêtoru-hodo massugu itte-kudasai.

How can I get to the museum?

Bijutsu-kan-e-wa dô-ike-ba-ii-desu-ka.

Come *along with* me. I'll show you.

Watashi-*to-issho-ni* kite-kudasai. Go-annai-shi-masu.

Excuse me, but where is the public library?

Sumimasen-ga, kôritsu-tosho-kan-wa doko-ni-ari-masu-ka.

Go down this street and turn to the left at the first intersection.

Kono michi-o massugu itte, saisho-no kôsa-ten o hidari-e magatte-kudasai.

Could you tell me the way to the hospital?

Byôin-e-iku michi-o **oshiete-itadake-masen-ka**.

Go over the bridge over the road **and** you'll see a brick building on your left. That's the hospital.

Ôdan-hodô-kyô-o **watatta-ra** hidari-te-ni renga-no tatemono ga mie-masu. Sore-ga byôin-desu.

Is this the right way to the bank?

Ginkô-e-wa **kono michi de ii-no-desu-ka**.

Yes, madam, you are correct.

Hai, (oku-san), sô-desu.

No, sir, you are *quite* wrong.

Iie, (anata), *zenzen* chigai-masu.

I'll draw a rough map for you.

Ryakuzu-o kaite-age-mashô.

Excuse me, could you tell me where the restroom is?

Sumimasen-ga, o-tearai-wa doko-ka oshiete-itadake-masen-ka.

There's one on the 3rd floor, *beside* the stairs.

San-gai-no kaidan-*no-soba-ni* ikkasho ari-masu.

Excuse me, could you tell me where *the nearest* subway

station is?

Sumimasen-ga, *ichibân-chikai* chika-tetsu-no eki-wa doko-deshô.

Subway? It's about 1 kilometer and a half. You **might want** to take a taxi.

Chika-tetsu. Ichi-kiro-han-hodo-ari-masu. Takushî-ni no-rareta-ra **ikaga-deshô**.

Where am I now on this map?

Kono chizu-de genzai-chi-wa doko-deshô.

This is the place we are now.

Koko-ga ima watashi-tachi-ga iru tokoro-desu.

Is the theater *far* from here?

Gekijô-wa koko-kara *tooi*-desu-ka.

No, it takes *only* five minutes *by* bus.

Iie, basu-*de honno* go-fun-desu.

No, it's within a walking distance.

Iie, aruite-ikeru-kyori-desu.

Excuse me, is this the *nearest* way to the station?

Sumimasen-ga, eki-e-wa kore-ga *ichiban-chikai* michi-desu-ka.

No, you're wrong. **Go back** about 2 blocks **and** turn

right.

Iie, chigai-masu. Toori-o-futatsu **modotte**, migi-e magatte-kudasai.

15) At a station (Eki-de)

I'd like to go *to* the M Station. **Which** train should I take?

Emu-eki-*e* iki-tai-no-desu. **Dono** ressha-ni nore-ba-ii-desu-ka.

Take a train *for* S from Track 1.

Ichi-ban-sen-kara Esu-*iki-no* ressha-ni nottte-kudasai.

Is it a local train?

Sore-wa futsû-ressha-desu-ka.

Yes, but **if** you are *in a hurry*, take a limited express.

Ee, demo o-*isogi*-**nara**, tokkyû-ni notte-kudasai.

Take an express and *get off* at the I Station. *Then* transfer to a train for T.

Kyûkô-ni notte Ai-eki-de *orite-kudasai*. *Sore-kara* Tî-iki-no ressha-ni nori-kaete-kudasai.

Does this train stop at B Station?

Kono ressha-wa Bî-eki-ni tomari-masu-ka.

No, **I'm afraid not**. Take the next local train.

Iie, tomara-**nai-to-omoi-masu**. Tsugi-no futsû-sha-ni notte-kudasai.

How much does it cost to the museum?

Bijutsu-kan-made ikura-desu-ka.

The fare is 200 yen.

Ryôkin-wa nihyaku-en-desu.

Which station **should** I get off at?

Dono-eki-de ori-**nakereba-ike-masen**-ka.

At the C Station. Shî-eki-de-desu. or Shî-eki-de orite-kudasai.

How many stops are there from here?

Eki-no-kazu-wa koko-kara **ikutsu**-ari-masu-ka?

Six. Muttsu-desu.

Does this train have a restroom?

Kono ressha-ni-wa toire-ga-ari-masu-ka.

Yes, at the rear of the two cars *ahead*.

Hai, ni-ryô-*mae-no*-sharyô-no kôbu-ni-ari-masu.

Where is the bus terminal?

Basu-tâminaru-wa doko-desu-ka.

On the 2nd floor of that large building.

Ano ooki-na biru no ni-kai-*ni*(-ari-masu).

Does this bus go to E?

Kono basu-wa Î-e iki-masu-ka.

No, take No. 18 bus.

Iie, jû-hachi-keitô-no basu-ni notte-kudasai.

16) In a train (Shanai-de)

May I see your ticket?

Jôsha-ken-o haiken-deki-masu-ka.

Sir, where **are you going**?

Dochira-e **ikare-masu-ka**.

I'm going to the T Station.

Tî-eki-made iki-masu.

Sir, you **have to** pay …yen *extra*.

Tsuika-ryôkin …en-o o-harai-itadaka-**nakereba-nari-masen**.

17) Tickets (Kippu)

I'd like to make a reservation for your flight to Sapporo on 7/15.

Shichigatsu-jû-go-nichi Sapporo-iki(-hikô-ki)-no yoyaku-o-shi-tai-no-desu-ga.

We have one flight 685 leaving at 8:30

Hachi-ji-sanjuppun-hatsu roppyaku-hachijû-go-bin-ga-ari-masu.

2 Green Tickets for "Hikari 182" to Kyoto on 8/10.

Hachigatsu-tô-ka-no "Hikari-hyaku-hachijû-ni-gô"-no Gurîn-ken, Kyôto-made ni-mai-kudasai.

. . . .

I'd like to go to Karuizawa from the 3rd of May.

Gogatsu-mikka-kara Karuizawa-e iki-tai-no-desu-ga.

How many days would you like **to stay** there?

Nampaku-sare-masu-ka.

I'd like to have a two night stay there.

Ni-haku shi-tai-no-desu.

This is the "Golden Week" *the busiest* week in the year,

so **I'm not sure if** I could book you on a train or at a hotel. I'll give it a try, but . . .

Chôdo ima ichi-nen-jû-de, *ichiban konzatsu-suru* Gôruden-Wîku-desu-node, or Ima Gôruden-Wîku-deshite, ichi-nen-de *ichiban konzatsu-suru* shû-desu-kara, ressha ya hoteru no yoyaku-ga toreru-**ka-dô-ka-wakari-masen**, atatte-wa mi-masu-ga . . .

I got you a train ticket with reserved seat, but I'm sorry A Hotel has no rooms available.

Shitei-ken-wa tore-mashita-ga, zannen-nagara Ei-Hoteru-ni-wa aki-shitsu-ga-gozai-masen.

Oh, you're lucky! I got you a single-room at B Hotel.

A, o-kyaku-sama-wa un-ga-ii-desu-yo! Bî Hoteru-de shinguru-ga isshitsu tore-mashita.

Thank God! Do you accept this credit card?

Tasukatta! Kono kurejitto-kâdo-wa tsukae-masu-ka.

Sure. Kekkô-desu.

. . . .

Excuse me. Are there any tickets left for *tomorrow evening*?

Sumimasen. *Asu-no-ban*-no chiketto-ga ari-masu-ka.

Where would you like?

Dono-seki-o go-kibô-desu-ka.

S seats. Esu-seki-desu.

I'm afraid all the S seats are sold out. I have some A seats left.

Zannen-desu-ga Esu-seki-wa subete uri-kire-mashita. Ei-seki-wa sukoshi nokotte-i-masu.

How much are they? Ikura-desu-ka.

5,000 yen for adults and 3,000 yen for children.

Otona go-sen-en, kodomo san-zen-en-desu.

Give me two for adults and three for children.

Otona ni-mai kodomo san-mai-kudasai.

What time does the performance begin?

Ensô-wa nanji-ni hajimari-masu-ka.

It begins at 6:30.

Roku-ji sanjuppun-ni hajimari-masu.

18) Doing the sights (Kankô)

Please tell me some interesting places in Tokyo.

Tôkyô-no meisho-o **oshiete-kudasai**.

The Meiji Shrine, Shiba Park, the Imperial Palace *and so on*. **You'd better take** a sightseeing bus.

Meiji-jingû, Shiba-kôen, Kôkyo-*nado*-desu. Kankô-basu-ni **no-rareru-hô-ga-ii-desu**-yo.

How long does it take to do the sights of Tokyo by bus?

Basu-de Tôkyô-kankô-o suru-noni dore-kurai jikan-ga-kakari-masu-ka.

It takes about 8 hours. The bus fare is ...yen.

Yaku hachi-jikan kakari-masu. Ryôkin-wa ...en-desu.

How often does the sightseeing bus leave *every day*?

Kankô-basu-wa *mai-nichi* **nankai** dete-i-masu-ka.

Every four hours, from Tokyo Station.

Yo-jikan-*oki-ni* Tôkyô-eki-kara dete-i-masu.

Does the bus guide explain *in* English?

Basu-gaido-san-wa Eigo-*de* setsumei-shite-kure-masu-ka.

Yes, she does. Hai, shite-kure-masu.

. . . .

Have you been *to* Kyoto?

Kyôto-*e* **itta-koto-ga-ari-masu-ka**.

Yeah, I've been there *three times* to do the sights. I'd like to go to some countryside and stay *for* a week.

Ee. Kyôto-e-wa kankô-de *san-do* iki-mashita. Doko-ka chihô-e itte isshû-*kan* taizai-shite-mi-tai-desu.

Then, I'll take you to some quiet place **you've never been** *before*.

Sore-jâ, anata-ga *ima-made* **itta-koto-no-nai** shizuka-na tokoro-ni o-tsure-shi-mashô.

Where are you going?

Doko-e iku-no-desu-ka.

Mizuo in Kyoto. Kyôto-no Mizuo-desu.

It **must be** *way out of* regular sightseeing courses.

(Sore-wa) Futsû-no kankô-kôsu-*kara* *(zutto)* *hazurete*-iru-ni-**chigai-nai**.

That's correct. Sô-nan-desu.

Do you see those houses *with* lattice doors?

Kôshi-do-*no-aru* ie-ga mie-masu-ka?

Yes. Ee.

They're stores selling pickles and sweets.

Asoko-wa tsukemono ya kashi-o utte-iru mise-na-n-desu.

Here we are *in* Hozukyo.

Sâ, Hozukyô-*ni* **tsuki-mashita**.

What a beautiful river it is! What **is** it **called**?

Nan-to utsukushii kawa-desu-ne! Nan-**to-iu** kawa-desu-ka.

It's Hozu River which is quite famous *in* Japan.

Nihon-*de* totemo yûmei-na Hozu-gawa-desu.

It's quite chilly. **Let's get** in bus *quick*.

Kanari hie-masu-ne. *Hayaku* basu-ni **nori-mashô**.

This is Mizuo: our destination.

Kore-ga Mizuo-de, wareware-no mokuteki-chi-desu.

Clean and fresh air is quite a treat *for* city people like us, isn't it?

Sumi-kitta shinsen-na kûki-wa wareware-no-yô-ni machi-ni-sunde-iru-mono-*ni-totte-wa* go-chisô-desu-ne.

You stay here *for a few days* and take a bath with citrons. I guarantee you long life.

Koko-ni *ni-san-nichi* toma-rare-te yuzu-no-haitta-furo-ni o-hairi-nasai. Naga-iki-deki-masu-yo.

That's great! Sore-wa subarashii!

I hope you'll visit us again **when** it's nice and warm.
Atatakaku-te jikô-no-ii-**toki-ni** mata o-ide-kudasai.

I *sure* would like that.
Hontô-ni sô shi-tai-mono-desu.

Why don't you take a boat ride down the river *then*?
Sono-toki-ni-wa fune-ni-notte kawa-kudari-o-shita-**ra dô-deshô**.

How splendid! Subarashii-desu-ne!

19) Cars (Kuruma)

Let's rent a car and drive to Hakone.
Kuruma-o kari-te Hakone-made doraibu-shi-yô.

Oh, no, we're running out of gas.
Oya, gasorin-ga naku-nari-sô-da.

Fill it up with regular.
Regyurâ man-tan.

The traffic is really bad today.
Kyô-wa honto-ni dôro-jijô-ga-warui-ne.

The radio says that there's about four kilometers of cars *bumper to bumper* at the ...ramp.

Rajio-de-wa …rampu-de yon-kiro-no-*jûtai*-da-to itte-ru-yo.

There was an accident here yesterday.

Kinô koko-de jiko-ga-atta-n-da.

What accident was it?

Donna jiko-datta.

It was a fender-bender. Tsuitotsu-jiko-datta.

It was a head-on collision.

Shômen-shôtotsu-datta.

The car slipped *because of* the snow.

Kuruma-ga yuki-*no-tame-ni* surippu-shita.

I **wonder if** I can find a back road.

Nuke-michi-ga nai-**ka-shira**.

20) A photograph (Shashin)

Could you take my picture?

(Watashi-no) Shashin-o totte-itadake-masu-ka.

Do I *just* push the shutter?

Shattâ-o osu-*dake*-desu-ka.

May I take pictures *in* this building?

Kono tatemono-*no-naka-de* **shashin-o totte-mo-ii-desu-ka**.

OK. Ii-desu-yo.

How about a flash? Furasshu-wa dô-desu-ka.

No, I'm afraid not.

Iie, ike-nai-to-omoi-masu.

I've run out of film for my camera. Where can I get a roll of film?

Firumu-ga naku-natta. Firumu-wa doko-ni utte-i-masu-ka.

You can get it at the kiosk of the entrance.

Iriguchi no baiten-de kae-masu.

. . . .

I **want to have** this roll of twenty-four develop**ed** and **made** some prints. How much will it be?

Kono nijû-yon-mai-dori-no-firumu-o genzô(**-shite**) purinto-**shite-hoshii-no-desu**. Ikura-ni-nari-masu-ka.

The developing charge is 400 yen. The printing fee *for* an L-size print is 19 yen. **How would you like** your prints? Glossy or mat?

Genzô-dai-ga yon-hyaku-en. Eru-saizu-*no* purinto-dai-ga (ichi-mai) jû-kyû-en-desu. Purinto-wa **dô-itashi-mashô**. Tsuya-ari ka tsuya-keshi-no-dochira-ni-itashi-mashô.

Glossy prints, please.

Tsuya-ari-de-o-negai-shi-masu.

Do you want a white border on your prints?

Fuchi-ari-o go-kibô-desu-ka.

No, *without* a border. When can I pick them up?

Ie, fuchi-*nashi-de*. Itsu tori-ni-kure-ba yoroshii.

They'**ll be ready** by *tomorrow afternoon*.

Asu-no-gogo-made-ni-wa **deki-masu**.

Please enlarge these negatives.

Kono nega-o hiki-nobashite-kudasai.

Which size would you like to?

Dono saizu-ni na-sai-masu-ka.

Please enlarge *each* of the negatives to cabinet size.

Kono naga-o (*sore-zore*) kyabine-ban-ni hiki-nobashi-te-kudasai.

21) Meals (Shokuji)

Let's dine out *this evening*.
Komban-wa gaishoku-shi-mashô.

Where shall we go *for* dinner?
Doko-e (yûshoku-o-)*tabe-ni*-iki-mashô-ka.

I'**ve the reservation** for Japanese restaurant.
Ryôtei-ni **yoyaku-o shite-ari-masu**.

What kind of food would you like?
Donna ryôri-ga tabe-tai-desu-ka.

I'd like to have a good "Sukiyaki."
Oishii "Sukiyaki"-ga tabe-tai.

I'd like to have a broiled "Unagi."
Unagi-no kaba-yaki-ga tabe-tai.

. . . .

Do you know any good restaurant *around* here?
Kono-*atari-de* ii resutoran-o go-zonji-desu-ka.

I recommend the ". . . . ."
". . . . ."-o o-susume-shi-masu.

Is it far from here?

Koko-kara tooi-desu-ka.

No, it's *near* the station.

Iie, eki-*no-chikaku*-desu.

. . . .

May I take your order, please?

Go-chûmon-o o-kiki-shi-mashô-ka.

May I have a menu?

Menyû-o misete-kure-masu-ka.

Would you let me know when you've decided?

O-kimari-ni-nari-mashita-ra o-shirase-kudasai-masu-ka.

Please serve me potage, *first.*

Hajime-ni potâju-o kudasai.

Would you like something to drink?

O-nomi-mono-wa.

Whisk(e)y and water, please.

Uisukî to mizu-o.

Which would you **prefer**, rice or bread?

Raisu to pan to **dochira-ga yoroshii**-desu-ka.

Two slices of toast.
Tôsuto-o ni-mai.

Do you have coffee *with* your meal?
O-shokuji-*to-issho-ni* kôhî-o meshi-agari-masu-ka.

I'll have coffee *later.*
Kôhî-wa *ato-de* kudasai.

Would you like to get some more coffee?
Kôhî-no o-kawari-wa-ikaga-desu-ka.

No, thank you. Could I have the bill?
Iya-kekkô-desu. O-kanjô-o o-negai-shi-masu.

This is my treat.
Kyô-wa watashi-no ogori-desu.

Let's split the tab.
Wari-kan-de iki-mashô.

I'll buy your dinner.
Yûshoku-o ogori-mashô.

22) Shopping (Kai-mono)

What can I do for you?
Irasshai-mase.

I'm just looking, thank you.

Chotto miteiru-dake-desu, (arigatô).

Excuse me, but where are stationary goods sold?

Sumimasen-ga, bumbôgu-wa doko-de utte-i-masu-ka.

They are sold *on* the south side of that east stairway over there.

Bumbôgu-wa achira-no higashi-kaidan no minami-gawa-*de* utte-i-masu.

What floor are the shoes on?

Kutsu-wa nan-gai-ni ari-masu-ka.

They are sold on the 5th floor.

(Kutsu-wa) Go-kai-de utte-i-masu.

Please ask in the traveling bags section. There is a salesgirl who can understand and speak English *well.*

Ryokô-kaban-no-kônâ-de o-tazune-kudasai. Soko-ni-wa Eigo-no-*yoku*-wakaru joshi-ten'in-ga ori-masu.

Please come this way. Kochira-e dôzo.

. . . .

Do you have a whisky *of. . .make* in stock?

. . .sei-no uisukî-ga ari-masu-ka.

Yes, we do. Hai, gozai-masu.

I'm sorry it's *out of stock* now.

Sumimasen-ga ima *kirashite*-ori-masu.

But **if** I phone the dealer, he can send one over by tomorrow morning.

Desu-ga dîrâ-ni denwa-itashi-masu-**to**, asu-no-asa-made-ni-wa hairi-masu.

I'll let you know **as soon as** I get it. Please write your name and phone number *right here.*

Hairi-**shidai** o-shirase-itashi-masu. *Koko-ni* o-namae to denwa-bangô-o o-kaki-kudasai.

They are sold out.

Uri-kire-mashita.

. . . .

Do you have . . . in stock?

. . . ga ari-masu-ka?

What price range did you have in mind?

Go-yosan-wa ikura-kurai-deshô-ka.

Don't you have anything *around* . . . yen?

. . . yen-*kurai*-no-ga ari-masen-ka.

These are . . . yen.

Kochira-de . . . en-ni-nari-masu.

That's *too* expensive. Don't you have anything *cheaper*?

Sore-wa taka-*sugi*-masu. *Motto-yasui*-no-wa arimasen-ka.

Can you make any reduction?

Sukoshi makete-kure-masu-ka.

No, our prices are all fixed.

Iie, subete teika-to-natte-ori-masu.

. . . .

Will ordinary wrapping be *all right*?

Futsû-no hôsô-de *yoroshii*-desu-ka.

No, gift-wrap, please. This is my gift card.

Iya, purezento-yô-no-tsutsumi-ni shite-kudasai. Kore-ga gifuto-kâdo-desu.

Will it be all right to wrap them *together*?

Issho-ni tsutsu-n-demo yoroshii-desu-ka.

No, please wrap them *separately*.

Iie, *betsu-betsu-ni* tsutsu-n-de-kudasai.

. . . .

Can you have them **delivered**?

(Sore-ra-o) **Haitatsu-shite-morae-masu-ka**.

Yes, I can. Hai, itashi-masu.

When can you have them delivered?

Itsu haitatsu-shite-morae-masu-ka.

Sometime tomorrow afternoon. Will that be convenient?

Asu-no gogo-ni-nari-masu. Sore-de yoroshii-desu-ka.

Yes, that'll be fine. Any delivery charge?

Ee, (sore-de) kekkô-dasu. Haitatsu-ryô-wa (o-ikura-desu-ka).

Two hundred yen *per* one pack.

Ikko(*-ni-tsuki*) nihyaku-en-desu.

Will you send this blouse to the U.S.A.? How much is it?

Kono burausu-o Amerika-e okutte-itadake-masu-ka. O-ikura.

15,000 yen, madam. The consumption tax and package charge will be *extra*.

Ichiman-gosen-en-desu, (oku-sama). Shôhi-zei to

hôsô-dai-wa *betsu-ni*-nari-masu.

Do you accept this credit card?

Kono kâdo-wa-tsukae-masu-ka.

Sure. May I have your signature here?

Kekkô-desu. Koko-ni go-shomei-kudasai-masu-ka.

I'd like to pay it *in installments.*

Bunkatsu-barai-ni-shi-tai-no-desu.

All right. Shôchi-itashi-mashita.

I'm sorry to have kept you waiting. I'll hand your credit card back. Here's a receipt.

O-matase-shite-sumimasen. (Kurejitto-)Kâdo-o o-kaeshi-itashi-masu. Reshîto-de-gozai-masu.

a) At a ladies' fashion section (Redîsu-fasshion-kônâ-de)

What color would you like?

Donna iro-o o-konomi-desu-ka.

How do you like this shirt?

Kono shatsu-wa ikaga-desu-ka.

May I try it on?

Shichaku-shite-mo-yoroshii-ka.

Please. This color looks very nice on you.

Dôzo. Kono iro-wa totemo *o-niai-desu*.

You don't think it's conservative?

Jimi-ja-nai-ka-shira.

It's too loud. Hade-sugi-masu.

This shirt is *a little bit* tight.

Kono shatsu-wa *sukoshi* kyûkutsu-desu.

The sleeves **seem** a little long.

Sode-ga sukoshi nagai-**yô-desu**.

It suits me *perfectly.*

Pittari-da-wa.

Do you have this size in different colors?

Kono-saizu-de iro-chigai-no-ga-ari-masu-ka.

I don't like the design.

Dezain-ga ki-ni-iri-masen.

I'm looking for a blouse for my sister.

Imôto-ni burausu-o sagashite-imasu.

Do you know her size?

Saizu-o go-zonji-desu-ka.

She wears size M.
Emu-saizu-o kite-i-masu.

I'll take it. Sore-o morai-mashô.

I don't think I'll get it.
Sore-wa iri-masen.

b) At a shoes section (Kutsu-kônâ-de)

Please show me some boots.
Bûtsu-o misete-kudasai.

I take size 6 in the U.S.A.
(Watashi-wa) Amerika-de-wa saizu-roku-o haite-i-masu.

Mat I try them on?
Haite-mite-mo-yoroshii-ka.

They are too loose.
Ooki-sugi-masu.

They are a little tight.
Sukoshi kyûkutsu-desu.

How would you like these ones?
Kore-wa ikaga-desu-ka.

I'd like a little wider ones.

Mô-sukoshi haba-no-hiroi-no-ga ii-desu-ne.

23) Complaints (Kujô)

I'd like to have this camera repaired.

Kono kamera-o nao-shite-hoshii-no-desu.

What seems to be wrong with it?

Doko-ga warui-no-de-shô-ka.

The shutter would not be released.

Shattâ-ga ori-masen.

The winding mechanism fails to work *sometimes*.

Makitori-ga *toki-doki* umaku-iki-masen.

May I examine it?

Chotto tameshite-mi-mashô.

Will you leave it here for 2 or 3 days?

Ni-san-nichi azuka-rasete-itadake-masu-ka.

Do you have any guarantee?

Hoshô-sho-o o-mochi-desu-ka.

Yes, I do. I believe they'll repair it *for free*.

Hai, motte-i-masu. *Muryô-de* naoshite-itada-keruno-de-shô-ne.

Sure. **When** it's ready, I'll call you.

Mochiron-desu. Naori-mashita-**ra**, o-denwa-itashi-masu.

. . . .

Three days *ago* I bought this blouse, but I found it had stains. Will you give me another?

Mikka-*mae* kono burausu-o katta-no-desu-ga, shimi-ga tsuite-i-mashita. Betsu-no(-mono)-o itadaki-tai-no-desu.

Could you exchange it for *another* size?

Betsu-no saizu-to tori-kaete-itadake-masen.

Will you refund me the money?

Henkin-shite-itadake-masu-ka.

Sure. Do you have the receipt?

Yoroshû-gozai-masu. Reshîto-o o-mochi-desu-ka.

24) A phone (Denwa)

The phone **is ringing**.

Denwa-ga **natteiru**.

Can somebody get it!

Dare-ka denwa-ni dete!

Hello. Moshi-moshi.

Hello, this is Kimura home.
Moshi-moshi, Kimura-desu.

This is Nancy. Is Akiko-san there?
Watashi Nanshî-desu. Akiko-san irasshai-masu(-ka).

Hold on a moment, please. . . Akiko, your call from Nancy.
Shô-shô o-machi-kudasai. . . Akiko, Nanshî-kara denwa-yo.

a) The wrong number (Machigai-denwa)

Could I speak *with* Nancy?
Nanshî-*to* o-hanashi-shi-tai-no-desu-ga.

We don't have a Nancy here. **What number** did you dail?
Uchi-ni-wa Nanshîtte i-masen-ga. **Nan-ban-ni** o-kake-ni-nari-mashita.

341-8835. San-yon-ichi-no hachi-hachi-san-go-desu-ga.

I'm afraid you've got the wrong number.
Bangô-o o-machigae-jâ-nai-ka-shira.

b) Asking someone to leave a message (Dengon-irai)

Smith speaking. May I speak to Mrs. Kimura?

Sumisu-to-môshi-masu. Kimura-san-o o-negai-shi-masu.

Sorry, she'*s out* at the moment.

Môshi-wake-gozai-masen-ga, Kimura-wa tada-ima *gaishutsu-chû-desu.*

When do you expect her back?

Itsu o-kaeri-desu-ka.

I really don't know. Would you like to leave a message?

Chotto wakari-kane-masu. O-koto-zuke-o uketamawari-mashô-ka.

Please tell her Smith called her.

Sumisu-kara denwa-ga-atta-to o-tsutae-kudasai.

Does she have your number?

Kimura-wa anata-no denwa-bangô-o shitte-i-masu-ka.

I believe so. Go-zonji-da-to-omoi-masu.

c) Asking to call up someone (Yobi-dashite-morai-tai-toki)

This is Haruki Nakamura. May I speak to Mr. Rogers?

Nakamura Haruki-to-môshi-masu. Rojâsu-san-o o-negai-shi-masu.

I'm sorry Rogers is on another phone.

Môshi-wake-gozai-masen-ga, Rojâsu-wa betsu-no denwa-de hanashi-chû-desu.

Do you think it's going to be long?

Nagaku-nari-sô-desu-ka.

I don't think so.

Sonna-koto-wa-nai-to-omoi-masu.

Oh, I'll hold then. Ja, machi-mashô.

d) When wishing to know the phone number (Denwa-bangô-o shiri-tai-toki)

Hello, could you give me the number for Daisuke Nakata *on* Chitose-cho, Chuo-ku?

Moshi-moshi, Chûô-ku, Chitose-chô-*no* Nakata

Daisuke-san no bangô-o oshiete-itadaki-tai-no-desu-ga.

Hold the line, please.

Sono-mama o-machi-kudasai.

The number you asked for is 77-8487.

O-toi-awase-no bangô-wa nana-nana-no hachi-yon-hachi-nana-desu.

Thank you. Arigatô.

e) The public telephone (Kôshû-denwa)

How do you use the public telephone?

Kôshû-denwa-wa dô-yatte kake-reba-ii-desu-ka.

Lift the receiver and put in a 10 yen coin.

Juwa-ki-o-totte jû-en-kôka-o ichi-mai ire-nasai.

Or insert the telephone card in the direction of the arrow.

Mata-wa terehon-kâdo-o ya-jirushi-no-hôkô-ni ire-nasai.

At the sound of tone, push the number you want.

Bû-to-iu-oto-*ga-kikoeta-ra*, kake-tai bangô-o oshi-nasai.

Within the city, it'*s not necessary* to push the area code.

Shinai-nara, shigai-kyokuban-o osu-*hitsuyô-wa-arimasen.*

How long can you talk for 10 yen?

Jû-en-de dore-kurai hanase-masu-ka.

One minute. Ippun-desu.

Could you change this 100 yen coin for 10 yen coins? I want to use the public telephone.

Kono hyaku-en-kôka-o jû-en-kôka-ni kaete-moraemasu-ka. Kôshû-denwa-o kake-tai-no-desu.

25) Making an arrangement (Yakusoku)

Are you free this weekend?

Kon-shûmatsu aite-ru.

How about having dinner *with me*?

Yûshoku-o *issho-ni* tabe-nai.

How about at 6 in the evening?

Yûgata roku-ji-ni dô.

I'm free that day.

Sono hi-wa aite-ru-yo.

It's not convenient for me this weekend.
Kon-shûmatsu-wa tsugô-ga-warui-n-da.

I'm sorry I have another appointment.
Ainiku sen'yaku-ga atte-ne.

I'm looking forward to seeing you after such a long time.
Hisashi-buri-ni aeru-no-ga tanoshimi-da.

Where shall we meet? Doko-de au.

Well, how about at the usual coffee shop at 5?
Sô-da-ne, itsumo-no kissa-ten-de go-ji-ni-dô.

26) At the office (Jimu-sho-de)

Where are the papers? Don't you know?
Ano shorui-wa doko-e-itta. Kimi shi-ra-nai.

Sorry, I don't know.
Watashi-wa shiri-masen-ga.

Oh, **here they are**! A, **atta-atta**!

Please type these up *on* the word processor.
Wâpuro-*de* (kore-ra-o) taipu-shite-kudasai.

How is the condition of that word processor?
(Sono) Wâpuro no chôshi-wa-**dô**.

It works *very well.* It's compact and easy to use.

Totemo chôshi-ga-ii-desu. Kompakuto-desu-shi tsukai-yasui-desu.

Insert the paper. . . . .it's **better** to make wider space between lines.

Kami-o irete. . . . .gyô-kan-o mô-sukoshi aketa-**hô-ga-ii-yo**.

It doesn't work *well* today.

Kyô-wa *umaku* ugoki-masen.

I've lost all the data.

Dêta-ga zembu kiete-shimai-mashita.

Looking at the screen too long, my eyes are tired out.

Gamen-no-mi-sugi-de, me-ga tsukarete-shimai-mashita.

Please finish it by *tomorrow evening.*

(Sore) *Asu-no yûgata*-made-ni shi-agete-oite-kureru.

27) After work (Shigoto-no-ato-de)

I've *just* finished. Let's go and have a drink.

Yatto sunda. Nomi-ni-i-kô.

It's not good for you to drink on an empty stomach.
Sukippara-ni nomu-no-wa yoku-nai-yo.

Another mug of beer! Jokki *mô*-ippai!

It's *almost* time for the last train.
Soro-soro shûden-no jikan-da.

I had barhop at three places last night.
Yûbe-wa san-gen hashigo-o-shita.

I have a hangover with headache.
Futsuka-yoi-de atama-ga-itai-yo.

28) At a hospital (Byôin-de)

What can I do for you?
Dô nasai-mashita.

I have a stomachache.
I-ga itami-masu.

So you need to see the internal medicine doctor.
Dewa naika-desu-ne.

Is it your first visit to this hospital?
Kono byôin-e-wa hajimete-desu-ka.

Yes, it is. Hai, hajimete-desu.

Fill out this form, please. Do you have your health insurance card?

Kono yôshi-ni kinyû-shite-kudasai. Kenkô-hoken-shô-o o-mochi-desu-ka.

Yes, I do. Hai, motte-i-masu.

Please go to the internal medicine department on the 2nd floor and present these documents to the reception desk.

Ni-kai-no naika-e ikare-te mado-guchi-ni kono shorui-o dashite-kudasai.

Please wait at the waiting room *till* your turn comes.

Jumban-ga kuru-*made* machiai-shitsu-de o-machi-kudasai.

. . . .

Mr. Smith, please come in.

Sumisu-san, o-hairi-kudasai.

Good morning, doctor.

Sensei, ohayô-gozai-masu.

I'm sorry to hear that you have a stomachache.

I-ga ita-mareru-sô-desu-ne.

I've been suffering for *about* one week.

Isshû-kan-*hodo* itami-masu.

Would you please lie down there?
Soko-ni yoko-ni-natte-kudasai.

Does your stomach hurt you *all the time*?
Zutto (i-ga) itami-masu-ka.

Yes, it does. Hai, itami-masu.

Do you feel pain here? Koko-ga itami-masu-ka.

You'll have your stomach X-rayed.
I-no rentogen-o tori-mashô.

Can you come on Thursday?
Mokuyô-bi-ni kore-masu-ka.

Yes, I can. Hai.

Please refrain from eating or drinking *after* 8 Wednesday night.
Suiyô-bi-no hachi-ji-*ikô-wa* nani-mo tabe-zu nomanai-de-kudasai.

Don't smoke *either*. Tabako-*mo* yamete-kudasai-yo.

Thank you, doctor. Sensei, arigatô-gozai-mashita.

. . . .

Good morning, doctor.

Sensei, ohayô-gozai-masu.

May I help you?

Dô-nasai-mashita.

I seem to have caught a cold.

Kaze-o hiita-yô-desu.

I have a headache.

Zutsû-ga-shi-masu.

Are you running a temperature?

Netsu-ga ari-masu-ka.

The temperature was 37.6 in the morning.

Asa sanjû-shichi-do roku-bu-ari-mashita.

Take off your shirt, please.

Shatsu-o nuide-kudasai.

Breathe in. Out. Breathe in *more*. Out.

Iki-o-sutte. Haite. *Motto-ookiku*-iki-o-sutte. Haite.

Take a look at your throat.

Nodo-o misete-kudasai.

Hmmm, it's red. I'll put some medicine in.

Fûn, akai-desu-ne. Kusuri-o nutte-oki-mashô.

Don't take a bath *for a while.*

Shibaraku nyûyoku-shi-nai-de-kudasai.

Come back daily two or three days.

Ni-san-nichi kayotte-kudasai.

I'll give you medicine *for* 5 days.

O-kusuri-o itsuka-*bun* dashite-oki-masu.

Please take it *both* before *and* after meal.

Shokuzen(*-to*) shokugo-ni nonde-kudasai.

These pills are for your throat.

Kono jôzai-wa nodo-no(-o)-kusuri-desu.

Don't chew them and let them melt in your mouth.

Kama-nai-de kuchi-no-naka-de namete-kudasai.

I am not good at taking these pills.

Watashi-wa kono jôzai wa niga-te-na-no-desu.

It always makes me sick at my stomach.

Itsu-mo i-o arashi-masu.

OK, then, you don't have to take them.

Sô-desu-ka, sore-jâ, o-nomi-ni-nara-naku-te-mo-ii-desu.

Instead, gargle very well.

Sono-kawari-ni shikkari ugai-o-shite-kudasai.

Pay the bill *at* window No. 8.

Hachi-ban-mado-guchi-*de* kaikei-o sumasete-kudasai.

Turn in this numbered tag for your medicine, please.

Kono bangô-fuda-to-hiki-kae-ni o-kusuri-o o-watashi-shi-masu.

Thank you very much, doctor.

Sensei, dômo arigatô-gozai-mashita.

29) At the post office (Yûbin-kyoku-de)

Ten 80 yen stamps, please.

Hachijû-en-kitte-o jû-mai kudasai.

I'd like to send this letter registered.

(Kono tegami-o) Kakitome-de-o-negai-shi-masu.

I'd like to send this letter *by special delivery*.

(Kono tegami-o) *Sokutatsu-de* o-negai-shi-masu.

I'd like to send this card to the U.S. by air mail.

Kono kâdo-o kôkû-bin-de Amerika-e okuri-tai-no-desu-ga.

Is a letter in it?

Naka-ni tegami-ga-haitte-i-masu-ka.

No, just a card. Iie, kâdo-dake-desu.

I'd like to send this package to the U.S. *by surface mail.*

Kono kozutsumi-o *funa-bin-de* Amerika-e okuri-tai-no-desu-ga.

I'd like to send the cash by registered mail.

Genkin-kakitome-o-okuri-tai-no-desu.

What is the value of the content?

Ikura haitte-i-masu-ka.

30,000 yen.

Samman-en-haitte-i-masu.

Please give me 3,000 yen money order.

Sanzen-en-no ko-gawase-o kudasai.

What is the fee?

Tesûryô-wa ikura-desu-ka.

The way of counting the objects

The numerals and numeration

There are two ways of reading numbers; one derived from Chinese, the other handed down from classical Japanese. The numbers from one to ten may be read in both ways, but eleven and over may be read only in the former way.

	The way of reading derived from Chinese;	The way of reading handed down from classical Japanese;
1	ichi	hitotsu
2	ni	futatsu
3	san	mittsu
4	shi or yon	yottsu
5	go	itsutsu
6	roku	muttsu
7	shichi or nana	nanatsu
8	hachi	yattsu
9	ku or kyû	kokonotsu
10	jû	tô
11	jû-ichi	
12	jû-ni	
13	jû-san	
14	jû-shi or jû-yon	

15 jû-go
16 jû-roku
17 jû-shichi or jû-nana
18 jû-hachi
19 jû-ku or jû-kyû
20 nijû
21 nijû-ichi
22 nijû-ni
23 nijû-san
30 sanjû
34 sanjû-shi or sanjû-yon
35 sanjû-go
40 yonjû
50 gojû
60 rokujû
70 shichijû or nanajû
80 hachijû
90 kyûjû
100 hyaku
110 hyaku-jû
115 hayaku-jû-go
200 nihyaku
220 nihyaku-nijû
229 nihyaku-nijû-ku or nihyaku-nijû-kyû
300 sambyaku
400 yonhyaku

500	gohyaku
600	roppyaku
700	nanahyaku
800	happyaku
830	happyaku-sanjû
837	happyaku-sanjû-nana
900	kyûhyaku
940	kyûhyaku-yonjû
948	kyûhyaku-yonjû-hachi
1,000	sen
1,159	sen-hyaku-gojû-ku
2,000	nisen
3,000	sanzen
4,000	yonsen
5,000	gosen
6,000	rokusen
6,345	rokusen-sambyaku-yonjû-go
7,000	nanasen
8,000	hassen
9,000	kyûsen
10,000	ichiman
15,689	ichiman-gosen-roppyaku-hachijû-ku
20,000	niman
30,000	samman
40,000	yomman
50,000	goman

60,000 rokuman
70,000 nanaman
80,000 hachiman
90,000 kyûman
100,000 jûman
1,000,000 hyakuman

Ordinal numbers

1st dai-ichi(-no)
2nd dai-ni(-no)
3rd dai-san(-no)
4th dai-yon(-no)
5th dai-go(-no)
6th dai-roku(-no)
7th dai-nana(-no)
8th dai-hachi(-no)
9th dai-ku(-no)
10th dai-jû(-no)
11th dai-jû-ichi(-no)
12th dai-jû-ni(-no)
13th dai-jû-san(-no)
14th dai-jû-yon(-no)
15th dai-jû-go(-no)
16th dai-jû-roku(-no)
17th dai-jû-shichi(-no) or dai-jû-nana(-no)
18th dai-jû-hachi(-no)

19th dai-jû-ku(-no) or dai-jû-kyû(-no)
20th dai-nijû(-no)

Fractions

Fractions are indicated by inserting "-bun-no-" between a denominator and a numerator.

1/2	ni-bun-no-ichi
1/3	san-bun-no-ichi
2/3	san-bun-no-ni
1/4	yon-bun-no-ichi
2/4	yon-bun-no-ni
3/4	yon-bun-no-san
1/5	go-bun-no-ichi
2/5	go-bun-no-ni
3/5	go-bun-no-san
4/5	go-bun-no-yon
1/6	roku-bun-no-ichi
1/7	nana-bun-no-ichi
1/8	hachi-bun-no-ichi
1/9	kyû-bun-no-ichi
1/10	jû-bun-no-ichi
1/20	nijû-bun-no-ichi
1/50	gojû-bun-no-ichi
1/100	hyaku-bun-no-ichi
1/1000	sen-bun-no-ichi

Decimals

A decimal point is read as "-ten-."

10.5 jutten-go
9.6 kyû-ten-roku
8.7 hachi-ten-nana
7.8 nana-ten-hachi
6.9 roku-ten-kyû
5.0 gô-ten-zero
4.1 yon-ten-ichi
3.2 san-ten-ni
2.3 nî-ten-san
1.4 ichi-ten-yon
0.5 rei-ten-go
0.66 rei-ten-roku-roku
0.754 rei-ten-nana-go-yon
0.8765 rei-ten-hachi-nana-roku-go
0.0001 rei-ten-rei-rei-rei-ichi

No. . . .

No. 1 dai-ichi(-ban)
〃 2 dai-ni(-ban)
〃 3 dai-san(-ban)
〃 4 dai-yon(-ban)

〃	5	dai-go(-ban)
〃	6	dai-roku(-ban)
〃	7	dai-nana(-ban)
〃	8	dai-hachi(-ban)
〃	9	dai-kyû(-ban)
〃	10	dai-jû(-ban)
〃	11	dai-jû-ichi(-ban)
〃	12	dai-jû-ni(-ban)
〃	15	dai-jû-go(-ban)
〃	50	dai-gojû(-ban)
〃	100	dai-hyaku(-ban)

A time, times

a time or once ichi-do
twice ni-do : ni-bai
three times san-do : san-bai
four times yo-do : yo-bai
five times go-do : go-bai
six times roku-do : roku-bai
seven times nana-do : nana-bai
eight times hachi-do : hachi-bai
nine times ku-do : kyû-bai
ten times jû-do : jû-bai

Year(s)

1 year	ichi-nen
2 years	ni-nen
3 〃	san-nen
4 〃	yo-nen
5 〃	go-nen
6 〃	roku-nen
7 〃	shichi-nen or nana-nen
8 〃	hachi-nen
9 〃	kyû-nen or ku-nen
10 〃	jû-nen
11 〃	jû-ichi-nen
12 〃	jû-ni-nen
50 〃	gojû-nen
100 〃	hyaku-nen

this year	kotoshi
last year	kyonen
next year	rainen

Four seasons

spring haru

this spring kotoshi-no haru

summer natsu

last summer kyonen-no natsu

autumn aki

next autumn rainen-no aki

winter fuyu

this winter kotoshi-no fuyu

Month(s)

1 month	ikkagetsu or hito-tsuki
2 months	ni-ka-getsu or futa-tsuki
3 〃	san-ka-getsu or mi-tsuki
4 〃	yon-ka-getsu or yo-tsuki
5 〃	go-ka-getsu
6 〃	rokkagetsu or han-toshi
7 〃	nana-ka-getsu
8 〃	hachi-ka-getsu
9 〃	kyû-ka-getsu or ku-ka-getsu
10 〃	jukkagetsu
11 〃	jû-ikkagetsu
12 〃	jû-ni-ka-getsu or ichi-nen

this month kongetsu

last month sengetsu

next month raigetsu

Twelve months of the year

January ichigatsu

February nigatsu
March sangatsu
April shigatsu
May gogatsu
June rokugatsu
July shichigatsu
August hachigatsu
September kugatsu
October jûgatsu
November jûichigatsu
December jûnigatsu

Week(s)

(for) 1 week	isshû(-kan)
(〃) 2 weeks	ni-shû(-kan)
(〃) 3 〃	san-shû(-kan)
(〃) 4 〃	yon-shû(-kan)

this week	konshû
last week	senshû
next week	raishû

Date

1st day	tsuitachi
2nd 〃	futsuka

3rd	〃	mikka
4th	〃	yokka
5th	〃	itsuka
6th	〃	muika
7th	〃	nanuka
8th	〃	yooka
9th	〃	kokonoka
10th	〃	tôka
11th	〃	jû-ichi-nichi
12th	〃	jû-ni-nichi
13th	〃	jû-san-nichi
14th	〃	jû-yokka
15th	〃	jû-go-nichi
16th	〃	jû-roku-nichi
17th	〃	jû-shichi-nichi
18th	〃	jû-hachi-nichi
19th	〃	jû-ku-nichi
20th	〃	hatsuka
21st	〃	nijû-ichi-nichi
22nd	〃	nijû-ni-nichi
23rd	〃	nijû-san-nichi
24th	〃	nijû-yokka
25th	〃	nijû-go-nichi
26th	〃	nijû-roku-nichi
27th	〃	nijû-shichi-nichi
28th	〃	nijû-hachi-nichi

29th	〃	nijû-ku-nichi
30th	〃	sanjû-nichi
31st	〃	sanjû-ichi-nichi

Today, yesterday, tomorrow

today	kyô
yesterday	kinô
tomorrow	asu or ashita
morning	asa
afternoon	gogo
evening	yûgata or ban
night	yoru
a.m.	gozen
p.m.	gogo
this morning	kesa
yesterdaty morning	kinô-no asa
tomorrow morning	asu-no asa or myôchô
this afternoon	kyô-no gogo
yesterday afternoon	kinô-no gogo
tomorrow afternoon	asu-no gogo
tonight	komban or kon'ya
last night	sakuban or sakuya
tomorrow night	asu-no ban or myôban
the day before yesterday	ototoi
the day after tomorrow	asatte

Weekdays

Monday	getsuyô(-bi)
Tuesday	kayô(-bi)
Wednesday	suiyô(-bi)
Thursday	mokuyô(-bi)
Friday	kin'yô(-bi)

Weekend

Saturday	doyô(-bi)
Sunday	nichiyô(-bi)

this Wednesday	konshû-no suiyô(-bi)
last Thursday	senshû-no mokuyô(-bi)
next Friday	raishû-no kin'yô(-bi)

Hour(s)

1 hour	ichi-jikan
2 hours	ni-jikan
3 〃	san-jikan
4 〃	yo-jikan
5 〃	go-jikan
6 〃	roku-jikan
7 〃	nana-jikan
8 〃	hachi-jikan

9	〃	ku-jikan
10	〃	jû-jikan
12	〃	jû-ni-jikan
24	〃	nijû-yo-jikan

Time or hour

1 a.m.	gozen	ichi-ji
2 〃	〃	ni-ji
3 〃	〃	san-ji
4 〃	〃	yo-ji
5 〃	〃	go-ji
6 〃	〃	roku-ji
7 〃	〃	shichi-ji or nana-ji
8 〃	〃	hachi-ji
9 〃	〃	ku-ji
10 〃	〃	jû-ji
11 〃	〃	jû-ichi-ji
noon		shôgo
1 p.m.	gogo	ichi-ji
2 〃	〃	ni-ji
3 〃	〃	san-ji
4 〃	〃	yo-ji
5 〃	〃	go-ji
6 〃	〃	roku-ji
7 〃	〃	shichi-ji or nana-ji

8 〃	〃	hachi-ji
9 〃	〃	ku-ji
10 〃	〃	jû-ji
11 〃	〃	jû-ichi-ji
12 a.m.	gozen	rei-ji

Minute(s)

1	minute	ippun
2	minutes	ni-fun
3	〃	sampun
4	〃	yompun
5	〃	go-fun
6	〃	roppun
7	〃	nana-fun
8	〃	hachi-fun
9	〃	kyû-fun
10	〃	juppun
11	〃	jû-ippun
12	〃	jû-ni-fun
15	〃	jû-go-fun
30	〃	sanjuppun
45	〃	yonjû-go-fun

Second(s)

1	second	ichi-byô

2	seconds	ni-byô
3	〃	san-byô
4	〃	yon-byô
5	〃	go-byô
6	〃	roku-byô
7	〃	nana-byô
8	〃	hachi-byô
9	〃	kyû-byô
10	〃	jû-byô
11	〃	jû-ichi-byô
12	〃	jû-ni-byô
15	〃	jû-go-byô
30	〃	sanjû-byô
45	〃	yonjû-go-byô

Length

Centimeter(s)

1	centimeter	issenchi
2	centimeters	ni-senchi
3	〃	san-senchi
4	〃	yon-senchi
5	〃	go-senchi
6	〃	roku-senchi
7	〃	nana-senchi

8	〃	hassenchi
9	〃	kyû-senchi
10	〃	jussenchi
11	〃	jû-issenchi
12	〃	jû-ni-senchi
50	〃	gojussenchi
100	〃	hyaku-senchi = ichi-mêtoru
105	〃	ichi-mêtoru-go-senchi
150	〃	ichi-mêtoru-gojussenchi

Meter(s)

1	meter	ichi-mêtoru
2	meters	ni-mêtoru
3	〃	san-mêtoru
4	〃	yon-mêtoru
5	〃	go-mêtoru
6	〃	roku-mêtoru
7	〃	nana-mêtoru
8	〃	hachi-mêtoru
9	〃	kyû-mêtoru
10	〃	jû-mêtoru
11	〃	jû-ichi-mêtoru
12	〃	jû-ni-mêtoru
50	〃	gojû-mêtoru
100	〃	hyaku-mêtoru

1000	〃	sen-mêtoru or ichi-kiro(-mêtoru)
10000	〃	ichiman-mêtoru or jukkiro(-mêtoru)

Kilometer(s)

1	kilometer	ichi-kiro
2	kilometers	ni-kiro
3	〃	san-kiro
4	〃	yon-kiro
5	〃	go-kiro
6	〃	rokkiro
7	〃	nana-kiro
8	〃	hachi-kiro
9	〃	kyû-kiro
10	〃	jukkiro
11	〃	jû-ichi-kiro
12	〃	jû-ni-kiro
50	〃	gojukkiro
100	〃	hyakkiro

Weight

Gram(s)

1	gram	ichi-guramu
2	grams	ni-guramu
3	〃	san-guramu
4	〃	yon-guramu

5	〃	go-guramu
6	〃	roku-guramu
7	〃	nana-guramu
8	〃	hachi-guramu
9	〃	kyû-guramu
10	〃	jû-guramu
11	〃	jû-ichi-guramu
12	〃	jû-ni-guramu
50	〃	gojû-guramu
100	〃	hyaku-guramu
1000	〃	sen-guramu or ichi-kiro(-guramu)

Kilogram(s)

1	kilogram	ichi-kiro
2	kilograms	ni-kiro
3	〃	san-kiro
4	〃	yon-kiro
5	〃	go-kiro
6	〃	rokkiro
7	〃	nana-kiro
8	〃	hachi-kiro
9	〃	kyû-kiro
10	〃	jukkiro
11	〃	jû-ichi-kiro
12	〃	jû-ni-kiro
50	〃	gojukkiro

100	〃	hyakkiro

1) -satsu is used to count the number of book(s), dictionary(dictionaries), magazine(s), etc.

1	book	issatsu-no hon
2	books	ni-satsu-no hon
3	readers	san-satsu-no rîda
4	dictionaries	yon-satsu-no jisho
5	notebooks	go-satsu-no nôto
6	telephone books	roku-satsu-no denwa-chô
7	magazines	nana-satsu-no zasshi
8	weeklies	hassatsu-no shûkan-shi
9	monthlies	kyû-satsu-no gekkan-shi
10	annuals	jussatsu-no nenkan-shi

2) -mai is used to count the number of plate(s), paper, leaf(leaves), shirt(s), ticket(s), etc.

1	plate	ichi-mai-no sara
2	plates	ni-mai-no sara
3	sheets of paper	san-mai-no kami
4	〃	yon-mai-no kami
5	leaves	go-mai-no ha
6	〃	roku-mai-no ha
7	shirts	nana-mai-no shatsu

8	undershirts	hachi-mai-no hadagi
9	blouses	kyû-mai-no burausu
10	tickets	jû-mai-no kippu

3) -hon is used to count the numebr of pencil(s), candle(s), knife(knives), cigarette(s), beer, tooth(teeth), etc.

1	pencil	ippon-no empitsu
2	ball-point pens	ni-hon-no bôrupen
3	crayons	sambon-no kureyon
4	candles	yon-hon-no rôsoku
5	trees	go-hon-no ki(jumoku)
6	〃	roppon-no ki(jumoku)
7	knives	nana-hon-no naifu
8	cigarettes	happon-no tabako
9	bottles of beer	kyû-hon-no bîru
10	teeth	juppon-no ha

4) -hai is used to count the number of tea, coffee, milk, wine, whisk(e)y, water, etc.

1	cup of tea	ippai-no o-cha or kôcha
2	cups of tea	ni-hai-no o-cha or kôcha
3	cups of coffee	sambai-no kôhî
4	〃	yon-hai-no kôhî

5	cups of milk	go-hai-no miruku
6	〃	roppai-no miruku
7	cups of soup	nana-hai-no sûpu
8	glasses of wine	hachi-hai-no wain
9	glasses of whisk(e)y	kyû-hai-no uisukî
10	glasses of water	juppai-no mizu

5) -hiki is used to count the number of dog(s), cat(s), mouse(mice), insect(s), etc.

1	dog	ippiki-no inu
2	dogs	ni-hiki-no inu
3	〃	sambiki-no inu
4	cats	yon-hiki-no-neko
5	〃	go-hiki-no neko
6	〃	roppiki-no neko
7	mice	nana-hiki-no hatsuka-nezumi
8	〃	hachi-hiki-no hatsuka-nezumi
9	insects	kyû-hiki-no konchû
10	〃	juppiki-no konchû

6) -wa is used to count the number of bird(s).

1	sparrow	ichi-wa-no suzume
2	sparrows	ni-wa-no suzume
3	〃	samba-no suzume

4	〃	yon-wa-no suzume
5	swallows	go-wa-no tsubame
6	〃	roku-wa-no tsubame
7	〃	nana-wa-no tsubame
8	〃	hachi-wa-no tsubame
9	cranes	kyû-wa-no tsuru
10	〃	juppa-no tsuru

7) -ken is used to count the number of house(s), shop(s), etc.

1	house	ikken-no ie
2	houses	ni-ken-no ie
3	〃	sangen-no ie
4	stores	yon-ken-no mise
5	〃	go-ken-no mise
6	restaurants	rokken-no resutoran
7	Japanese restaurants	nana-ken-no ryôtei
8	bakeries	hakken-no pan'ya
9	confectioneries	kyû-ken-no yô-gashi-ten
10	stationary shops	jukken-no bumbôgu-ten

8) -nin is used to count the number of person(s).

father	chichi
mother	haha

	grandfather	sofu
	grandmother	sobo
1	son	hitori-no musuko
2	daughters	futari-no musume
3	brothers	san-nin-no kyôdai
4	sisters	yo-nin-no shimai
5	uncles	go-nin-no oji
6	aunts	roku-nin-no oba
7	nephews	shichi-nin-no oi
8	nieces	hachi-nin-no mei
9	cousins	kyû-nin-no itoko
10	grandsons	jû-nin-no mago
11	granddaughters	jû-ichi-nin-no mago-musume
20	boys	nijû-nin-no shônen
30	girls	sanjû-nin-no shôjo
50	men	gojû-nin-no dansei
100	women	hyaku-nin-no josei

9) -dai is used to count the number of radio(s), TV(s), camera(s), typewriter(s), piano(s), refrigerator(s), car(s), etc.

1	radio	ichi-dai-no rajio
2	TVs	ni-dai-no terebi
3	cameras	san-dai-no kamera
4	typewriters	yon-dai-no taipuraitâ

5	telephones	go-dai-no denwa
6	pianos	roku-dai-no piano
7	electric refrigerators	nana-dai-no denki-reizô-ko
8	electric washing machines	hachi-dai-no denki-sentakki
9	vacuum cleaners	kyû-dai-no denki-sôji-ki
10	cars	jû-dai-no kuruma

10) -kai is used to count the number of floor(s).

1st floor	ikkai
2nd 〃	ni-kai
3rd 〃	sangai
4th 〃	yon-kai
5th 〃	go-kai
6th 〃	rokkai
7th 〃	nana-kai
8th 〃	hachi-kai
9th 〃	kyû-kai
10th 〃	jukkai
15th 〃	jû-go-kai
30th 〃	sanjukkai

11) -dan is used to count the number of stair(s).

1	stair	ichi-dan

2	stairs	ni-dan
3	〃	san-dan
4	〃	yo(n)-dan
5	〃	go-dan
6	〃	roku-dan
7	〃	nana-dan
8	〃	hachi-dan
9	〃	kyû-dan
10	〃	jû-dan
11	〃	jû-ichi-dan
12	〃	jû-ni-dan
50	〃	gojû-dan

12) -chaku is used to count the number of coat(s) and suit(s).

1	dress	doresu itchaku
2	evening dresses	ibuningu-doresu ni-chaku
3	silk dresses	shiruku-doresu san-chaku
4	coats	kôto yon-chaku
5	overcoats	ôba go-chaku
6	raincoats	reinkôto roku-chaku
7	blazers	burezâ nana-chaku
8	suits	sûtsu hatchaku
9	coats	kôto kyû-chaku
10	raincoats	reinkôto jutchaku

13) -soku is used to count the number of shoes and socks.

1	pair of shoes	kutsu issoku
2	pairs of shoes	kutsu ni-soku
3	〃	kutsu sanzoku
4	pairs of boots	bûtsu yon-soku
5	〃	bûtsu go-soku
6	pairs of socks	sokkusu roku-soku
7	〃	sokkusu nana-soku
8	pairs of stockings	sutokkingu hassoku
9	〃	sutokkingu kyû-soku
10	pairs of tennis shoes	tenisu-gutsu jussoku

The human body and medical care

Symptoms (Shôjô)

to have a headache zutsû-ga suru

to feel a chill samuke-ga suru

to have a fever(a slight fever) netsu(binetsu)-ga aru

I am always sneezing./ I can't stop sneezing.
Taezu kushami-ga deru.

to have a running nose hanamizu-ga deru

My nose is stopped up. Hana-ga tsumatta.

to have a nosebleed hanaji-ga deru

to have a cough seki-ga deru

to cough up phlegm(bloody phlegm) tan(kettan)-ga deru

to have a sore throat nodo-ga itai

to have a pain in the joint kansetsu-ga itamu

My pluse is rapid. Myaku-ga hayai.

to look pale kaoiro-ga warui

to have palpitation dôki-ga suru

to be shoft of breath ikigire-ga suru

I feel like choking./ to have difficulty in breathing Iki-gurushii.

I feel languid. Karada-ga darui.

to suffer from insomnia nemure-nai

to have no appetite shokuyoku-ga nai

My stomach feels heavy./ to lie heavy on the stomach I-ga motareru.

to belch geppu-ga deru
to have a stomachache i-ga itamu
to have a stomachache before a meal onaka-ga suku-to i-ga itaku-naru
to have heartburn muneyake-ga suru
to feel nauseated hakike-ga suru
to vomit/ to throw up ôto-suru
to vomit blood toketsu-suru
to be constipated bempi-suru
to have'nt had a bowel movement for 5 days itsuka-kan bentsû-ga nai
to have diarrhea geri-o suru
There is blood in my stool. Ben-ni chi-ga majiru.
to have bloody stool ketsuben-ga deru
to feel dizzy memai-ga suru
My urine is bloody. Ketsunyô-ga deru.
to have difficulty in urinating nyô-ga de-nikui
My urine is turbid. Nyô-ga nigoru.
to have a pain when I urinate nyô-o dasu-toki itai
to have a pain in the anus kômon-ga itai
to have no period gekkei-ga nai
My shoulders often get stiff. Yoku kata-ga koru.
to have a pain in the back senaka-ga itai
to suffer from lumbago koshi-ga itai
to have a swollen lymph node rimpasen-ga hareru
I have got a boil [on my back]. [Senaka-ni] Odeki-ga

dekiru.
My skin itches. Karada-ga kayui.
to break out in a rash hasshin-ga dekiru
My eyes itch. Me-ga kayui.
to have sore eyes me-ga itai
I got some sleep at the corner of my eyes. Meyani-ga deru.
to have a pain in the ear mimi-ga itai
to have a ringing in the ears miminari-ga suru
to have discharge from the ear(s) mimidare-ga deru
My mouth feels dry. Kuchi-ga kawaku.
to have bad breath kôshû-ga suru
to be hoarse koe-ga kasureru
to have a toothache ha-ga itai
My gums are bleeding. Haguki-kara chi-ga-deru.
My gums are swollen. Haguki-ga hareru.
(When I drink something cold) it makes my teeth ache.
(Tsumetai-mono-o nomu-to) ha-ni shimiru.
to sprain one's ankle ashikubi-o kujiku
to get a bruise daboku-suru
to have a burn(a scald) yakedo-suru
My legs are swollen. Ashi-ga mukumu.
My hands and legs are numb. Te-ashi-ga shibireru.
to fall into a fit of convulsions keiren-o okosu

Names of disease (Byômei)

acute kyûsei-no

an allergy arerugî
appendicitis chûsui-en
atopic dermatitis atopî-sei hifu-en
blood pressure ketsuatsu
a bone fracture kossetsu
bronchitis kikanshi-en
cerebral apoplexy nô-ikketsu
chicken pox mizu-bôsô
chronic mansei-no
cirrhosis of the liver kan-kôhen
a cold kaze
conjunctivitis ketsumaku-en
a contagious disease; an infectious disease; an epidemic
densen-byô
dislocation dakkyû
a faint kizetsu
food poisoning shoku-chûdoku
a gallstone tanseki
a gastric ulcer i-kaiyô
gastritis i-en
German measles; rubella fûshin
gout tsûfû
heart attack kyôshin-shô
heart trouble shinzô-byô
hepatitis A (B) Ei-gata (Bî-gata) kan-en
(a) hernia herunia

high blood pressure　kô-ketsuatsu
hives　jimma-shin
inflammation　enshô
influenza; the flu　ryûkan
an injury; a wound　kizu
low blood pressure　tei-ketsuatsu
the measles　hashika
(the) mumps　otafuku-kaze
myocardial [cardiac] infarction　shinkin-kôsoku
neuralgia　shinkei-tsû
(a) neurosis　noirôze
(a) pain　itami
pneumonia　hai-en
a pulled muscle　niku-banare
rheumatism　ryûmachi
a sprain　nenza
subarachnoid hemorrhage　kumomaku-shita shukketsu
tonsillitis　hentôsen-en
tympanitis　chûji-en

Medical vocaburaries (Iryô-yôgo)

a general hospital　sôgô-byôin
a medical (a doctor's) office/ a clinic　shinryô-sho
a [public] health center　hoken-sho
to see a doctor regularly/ to receive regular outpatient treatment　tsûin-suru

to go into a hospital nyûin-suru
to leave the hospital taiin-suru
a blood type ketsueki-gata
a medical certificate shindan-sho
[medical] treatment chiryô
an injection chûsha
recovery kaifuku
a relapse saihatsu
liquid food ryûdô-shoku

Names of hospital department (Kaku-kamai)

(the department of) internal medicine naika
raspiratory disease kokyûki-ka
candiology junkanki-ka
surgery geka
orthopedics seikei-geka
neurosurgery nô-shinkei-geka
esthesia masui-ka
radiology hôshasen-ka
psychiatry shinkei-ka
obstetrics and gyneology (dept.)/ OBS/GYN san-fujin-ka
pediatrics shôni-ka
urology (dept.) hinyôki-ka
dermatology hifu-ka
ophthalmology ganka
otolaryngology/ the ear, nose and throat dept./E.N.T. jibi-

inkô-ka
Dental/Oral Surgery shika
plastic surgery (cosmetic surgery) keisei-geka
new patient shoshin
pharmacy yakkyoku

About the human body (Jintai-yôgo)

the abdomen fuku-bu
the abdominal region kafuku-bu
the ankle kurubushi
the arm ude
the armpit waki-no-shita
the back senaka
the back part of the head kôtô-bu
the backbone sebone
blood chi
a bone hone
the brain nô
the breast(s) chibusa
the buttocks shiri
the calf fukurahagi
a cheek hoo
the chest mune
a constitution taishitsu
an ear mini
an earlobe mimi-tabu

an elbow hiji

an eye me

  an eyeball gankyû

  an eyebrow mayu; mayu-ge

  eyelashes matsuge

  an eyelid mabuta

a face kao

a finger yubi

  the thumb oya-yubi

  the index finger; the forefinger hitosashi-yubi

  the middle finger naka-yubi

  the third finger kusuri-yubi

  the little finger ko-yubi

a fist kobushi

the forehead hitai

frame taikaku

the genital organs seiki

hair kami-no-ke

a hand te

a head atama

the heel kakato

height shinchô

the human body jintai

a jaw ago

a joint kansetsu

a knee hiza

a leg; a foot ashi

the limbs te-ashi
a lip kuchibiru
a mouth kuchi
a muscle kinniku
a nail tsume
the navel heso
a neck kubi
a nerve shinkei
a nose hana
a nostril bikô
the palm of the hand te-no-hira
a rib rokkotsu
the shin sune
the shoulder kata
a shoulder blade kenkô-kotsu
the skin hifu
the skull zugai-kotsu
the temple komekami
a thigh futo-momo
the throat nodo
a toe ashi-no-yubi; tsuma-saki
a tongue shita
a tooth ha
the tympanic membrane komaku
the vocal cords seitai
the waist; the loin koshi

weight taijû
a wrist te-kubi

the anus kômon
the appendix môchô
an artery dômyaku
the bladder bôkô
a blood vessel kekkan
the bowels chô
a bronchus kikanshi
the diaphragm ôkaku-maku
the duodenum jûnishi-chô
the esophagus shokudô
the gallbladder tannô
the heart shinzô
the kidney jinzô
the large intestine daichô
the liver kanzô
the lungs haizô
an ovary ransô
the pancreas suizô
the prostate (gland) zenritsu-sen
the rectum chokuchô
the small intestine shôchô
the spleen hizô
the stomach i

the trachea kikan
a ureter nyôkan
the urethra nyôdô
a vein jômyaku
the womb shikyû

SECOND PUBLISHED IN OCT., 1996

Title: **How to speak Japanese**

Edited by Hiroshi Takahashi
Kyoko Takahashi

Chief editor Tomoko Honjô

Taiseido Shobo Co.

4-13 Aotani-cho 4-chome, Nada-ku, Kobe (657)

(Printed in Japan)

TAISEIDO'S PUBLICATIONS

* Pocket Romanized English-Japanese Dict.
  [Revised Expanded Edition]

* Pocket Romanized Japanese-English Dict.

* Pocket Romanized Japanese-English Dict.
  [Abridged Edition]

* Romanized English-Japanese Dict.
  Japanese-English
  [Pocket Size] (Revised Edition)

* How to speak Japanese

* How to speak Osaka Dialect